SECRETS
OF
A
BEAUTY
QUEEN

SECRETS OF A BEAUTY QUEEN

STEPHANIE DARLING

VIKING
an imprint of
PENGUIN BOOKS

VIKING

UK | USA | Canada | Ireland | Australia
India | New Zealand | South Africa | China

Penguin Books is part of the Penguin Random House group of companies
whose addresses can be found at global.penguinrandomhouse.com.

Penguin
Random House
Australia

First published by Penguin Random House Australia Pty Ltd, 2017

10 9 8 7 6 5 4 3 2 1

Text copyright © Stephanie Darling 2017

Cover and text design by Adam Laszczuk © Penguin Random House Australia Pty Ltd
Author photograph © Justin Ridler
Typeset in Fournier by Adam Laszczuk, Penguin Random House Australia Pty Ltd
Colour separation by Splitting Image Colour Studio, Clayton, Victoria
Printed in China by 1010 Printing International Ltd

National Library of Australia
Cataloguing-in-Publication data:

Secrets of a beauty queen / Stephanie Darling.
9780670079216 (paperback)
Darling, Stephanie.
Fashion editors – Australia – Biography.
Women journalists – Australia – Biography.
Beauty, Personal.

746.92092

penguin.com.au

CONTENTS

*For my
darling sons,
Harrison
&
Jonah,
who are
my greatest
beauty
creations.*

FOREWORD

I FIRST WORKED WITH STEPHANIE IN JULY 2001 when she came on board as the beauty director at *Harper's Bazaar* at Australian Consolidated Press. I was publishing director at the time and we spent many happy hours gossiping about makeup and working on beauty ideas for the readers. When the launch of *Madison* was about to become a reality, the intrepid Stephanie came immediately to mind. I remember us meeting for a manicure before work one morning and my asking her if she would join the team. It was an enthusiastic 'Yes'.

We kept in touch after I had left ACP and went to Fairfax Media, and when *Madison*, sadly, was closed, I asked Stephanie to take up the role of beauty director on *Sunday Life*. It was a contributor position but she insisted on working in the office every week. She loves involvement with the team and when she is not parading her latest shoe purchases she is regaling us with outlandish tales of extreme beauty procedures and her latest product obsessions. She now also works for our sister website *Daily Life* as their beauty director and contributes to *Good Weekend*.

We have been eagerly watching the progress of *Secrets of a Beauty Queen*. This book captures the intriguing world that is beauty, with must-have tips, lust-have products, behind-the-scenes peeks, and world travels, all woven together with her delightful sense of fun and humour, and shining with the passion she has for the industry she loves.

PAT INGRAM
Editorial Director of *Sunday Life*

*SECRETS OF
A BEAUTY
QUEEN*

INTRODUCTION

I HAVE REACHED THAT FUNNY AGE, 56, where for the first time in my life I am beginning to feel just the tiniest bit invisible. I've even started flirting with the possibility of a facelift, all in the name of science of course – the ultimate road test.

Manicured hands down, I have the best job in the world. I think you'll probably agree with me once I've told you some of the incredible and outlandish things I've done, all for the sake of beauty. I have worked on amazing magazines, including *Vogue* and *Harper's Bazaar* and now I have my very own column in the *Sun-Herald*'s colour supplement, *Sunday Life*, as well as an online presence with *Daily Life*. When I sat down with the editorial director to discuss the format of my column, we conceived 'the road test', which basically meant me putting my body on the line to test all sorts of weird and wonderful treatments.

To date, I have done 170 road tests. If there is a beauty treatment out there, odds are I've trialled it. They range from sublime facials and massages that have taken me to nirvana and back, to excruciating but highly effective treatments such as Ultherapy, to perfectly painted nails and toes (a pedicure really is a little slice of heaven), to having my hair coloured in Paris by the most famous colourist in the world. This, believe it or not, is my job.

There was a time in my early 20s, when I was just starting out in magazines, where I stated confidently that I would never have cosmetic surgery. I was young and it was the early 80s; if women were having procedures done they were very secretive about it. Times changed and I had a complete about-face in my mid-30s, trialling injectable lip filler for the first time, bruises and all. Now, whatever is out there (within reason, I might add), I am game to try it for research – and also to keep ageing at bay.

Appearance is important and a good hair day can make or break a deal. I always feel more confident if I am wearing my beloved makeup and a shot of my favourite fragrance. I am ludicrously lucky to have access to world-class makeup artists, hair stylists and colourists, skin-care experts, cosmetic and plastic surgeons, facialists, manicurists – and I have made full use of them.

The beauty industry is continually evolving and that's why I adore it. There are always new trends and expanding boundaries; outlandish, exotic, luxurious and down-to-earth treatments that can make a difference, whether they last an hour or a lifetime. I embrace it all – and filter it for my readers.

SECRETS OF
A BEAUTY
QUEEN

1

WORKING IT

*T*HE BEAUTY INDUSTRY HAS CHANGED RADICALLY since I started out at *Vogue* over 30 years ago. That day is burnt into my memory, as it set me on the path to seriously the best job in the world for me, bar none.

My wildest dream was to work at *Vogue Australia* and hoping beyond hope — I mean really, who did I think I was? — I wrote off eagerly into the ether and got a 'Thanks for the letter, we'll keep it on file' reply; I was gutted. I ended up taking up a graduate position with a legal publishing firm, where I worked on riveting titles such as the *Australian Criminal Law Reports* and a local government magazine called *The Shire and Municipal Record*. It was 1983 and the worst year of graduate employment on record. (Everyone who's ever graduated says that about their year, but really, it was!)

I was two years into the role when I met my mother's new English neighbour, who had moved into a terrace across the street in Paddington and was working at Condé Nast. She said that *Vogue Entertaining* was looking for a subeditor; she even managed to get me an interview. My god, I couldn't believe my luck. That connection, combined with a herculean amount of enthusiasm, got me through the door. I would have done anything to get that job, even licked the carpet if they had asked me to. However, the position ended up going to a more experienced journalist; I had none. So I settled back into my routine.

WORKING
IT

A month or so later, the managing editor of *Vogue Australia* called and asked me to come in to interview for a trainee subeditor role. *Are you kidding me?* I thought. I couldn't believe it. I did a subbing test that I remember vividly. It was a story about beauty royalty: the Lauder family of Estée Lauder fame. Prophetic, right? The heading I wrote for the piece was 'Praise the Lauders'. And so it all began . . .

I got the job. To this day, this fact still astonishes me. As you might have guessed, I have a highly developed case of imposter syndrome and back then it was set in overdrive. I think my boundless enthusiasm and desire to please, as well as my heading, got me over the line.

Day one: God, what to wear? From memory, I think it was a crimson-and-white spotted denim Moschino mini-skirt suit. It was the 80s, remember. To say that I was awestruck is beyond an understatement. June McCallum was our illustrious editor. She had what was known in the industry as 'the eye', an infallible ability to get it right, and this unnerving exactitude helped form me into the journalist I am today. June's trademark was an armful of exotic bangles that clacked together, so you always knew when she was on the approach. My colleagues in the *Vogue* stable were all legends in the making, including Karin Upton Baker (now managing director of Hermès Australia) and Edwina McCann (editor of *Vogue Australia*). We were all based in a building in Sydney's Clarence Street, complete with a lift driver and tea lady. Those were the days.

New girl stuff is always challenging and this first day was no different. I was given a desk and chair and when I went to sit down, discovered the chair was missing a leg. When I pointed this out to the business manager, who was famous for watching the pennies, she told me to just lean forward. I was all prepared to do just this when Shona Martyn, who was editor of the arts section (now publishing director of HarperCollins), sprang to my defence and insisted that I have a chair that functioned. From that moment Shona has been my mentor, and first and foremost a dear friend. She also gave me my first writing assignment, interviewing an a capella group. It was only 300 words but I couldn't believe it: I had my first piece published in *Vogue*.

I was the last trainee subeditor that *Vogue* took on and it was a baptism of fire. In 1985 magazines were produced using offset printing. The printer spat out galleys of the stories we had subbed that hopefully were word perfect, but, shock horror, there were sometimes spelling mistakes, which meant we had to get old galleys, trawl through them and find an instance of the word spelt correctly, cut it out and take it to the finished art department, who would then insert the correction. Next step was the finished boards, which had text pasted onto them and the film transparencies attached; these would then be sent to Hong Kong to be printed. We worked on a five-month lead time: let's just say, a lot can happen in five months. To this day there is nothing like the anticipation of receiving newly minted advance issues; this excitement is as sharp for me today as it was then. We would sit and look through the issues, evaluating what we were pleased with and what we could have done better, and wait to see how well they sold.

I worked very closely with Janette Cox, who was my surrogate mother at work and an absolute legend. She was a subeditor extraordinaire and one of the chicest women I know – and I know a lot of them. Janette had a magical way with words and a wicked sense of humour; she died in 2015 and I miss her terribly. This was my rigorous and

WORKING
IT

riotous training ground, where I learnt everything from the best in the business.

I was two years in to my first stint with *Vogue* when I was poached by Australian Consolidated Press. The largesse of the 80s was in full swing and I ended up working on the uproarious fashion broadsheet *Mode Magazine*. Lorraine Browne was our acute, perfectly pitched editor and Richard Walsh our publishing director, all under the big man, Kerry Packer. He was an astonishing boss to work for; demanding, yes, but also deeply loyal. One extreme example of this was when there was a bomb scare in the building. I looked up from my desk and saw Kerry Packer, who had come down personally to clear all the staff from every floor. Weirdly, I even remember what he was wearing that day: pink shirt and jeans. Quite stylish, really.

My role at *Mode* was twofold: I edited as well as subbed the beauty pages – my first taste of what was to become my absolute passion, beauty. *Mode* pushed the boundaries on absolutely everything. For the cover of one issue we even had a politician, the petite John Button, propped up on a box with a bevy of models. Our stable of incredibly talented writers included Andiee Paviour, who used to get right out there to field the most outlandish stories: riding as a hitchhiker with truckies crossing the Nullarbor and infiltrating a bikie gang, just to give two examples. Subbing her copy was always a highlight. It was here that I became adept at trimming copy without losing the flavour. In fact, starting out journalistic life as a subeditor has been invaluable for honing my writing skills.

I remember my very first beauty shoot: we shot a hair story with two models and Madonna's *Cherish* was playing in the background.

9

God, I loved that album. All good things come to an end, though. Lorraine ended up leaving *Mode* and I was offered a role on *Cleo* as its beauty and lifestyle editor. It seemed like a good idea at the time, but I was engaged to be married and when it came to working on the eligible bachelor campaign, my heart just wasn't in it.

Vogue then approached me to go back there to work as their copy director. On the day of my interview I had a splitting migraine but it felt like coming home. I was offered the job, said yes and got married the very next day. So it was back to my old haunt, now located at Greenwich on the north shore. The subbing was sustaining and the company delightful, but as a wise sub once said to me, it is a tricky role: 'It is incredibly responsible and demanding but with none of the kudos.' There is an element of truth to this and I was starting to want more, especially as I had had a taste of the beauty bounty and the possibilities that lay ahead.

In my second outing as a sub, though, there was one highlight: Baz Luhrmann and Catherine Martin were guest editors for our *Moulin Rouge* issue. I got to sit with Baz, who was seriously hypnotic and had a highly infectious work ethic, as we worked through the copy on the issue. I will never forget this experience.

There were some tumultuous times at *Vogue*. The British fashion luminary Marion Hume was appointed editor, and she really pushed the boundaries. This was an exciting time, as Marion shook up the fashion industry and created an incredibly lively and deeply demanding work environment. During that time, the beauty editor role became available. I had become so accustomed to my role that I had convinced myself this was where I would remain, pretty much forever. I will never forget the day

Marion liberated me. Thank you, Marion, from the bottom of my heart! She called me in to her office and said that she had just found out that I had worked as the beauty editor at *Mode* and would I take up the beauty editor position at *Vogue*? I was so taken aback that I said I would have to think about it. What was I thinking?

I went home and told my husband, who gasped and said, 'Why are we even having this conversation, of course you have to take it.' My old self-doubt had tripped me up again. I sprinted into Marion's office the next day yelling, 'Yes!' Working with Marion and the *Vogue* team was pure, unadulterated joy. I had my own office, including a sofa, and felt so grown-up, and the life of beauty and the never-ending flow of products began.

Peter Holder was editing *GQ* at the time and often visited my beauty enclave. He knew all my weaknesses, including my inability to share. I had been sent a Paddington Bear who I was very attached to – in fact, he still travels everywhere with me in my car – and Peter kept trying to make off with him. I came in one morning to find the bear gone and in its place a Polaroid photo featuring Paddington with his jumper pulled up over his eyes and a caption that said if I didn't pay up, 'The bear will get it.'

This role is where I learnt the fine art of editing and selecting which products would feature in the magazine. This is often a tough call. I am old school and consider the reader to be the number one priority; fortunately, one of the best things about beauty is that every brand has a hero. Nevertheless, the constant flow of products in every conceivable shape and size was sometimes overwhelming, and to this day I'm still learning to hone the selection process.

So my second stint at the *Vogue* mothership lasted ten exceptionally happy years and in that time I worked with a number of editors, including June McCallum, Nancy Pilcher, Marion Hume and Kirstie Clements. All had their unique take on what makes a magazine tick. Thank you one and all for an astonishing ride.

Next stop was editing and launching a brand-new title called *Australian Coastal Style*, little sister to *Country Style* magazine. I was approached by the publisher of FPC Magazines at the time, Michael McHugh, to come and work as the launch editor. Again, I was astonished that anyone would think I could be an editor. Michael and I had a hilarious first meeting where we talked about lots of things, including budgeting. I said I was not famous for that skill (just ask my husband) and he said it was just like balancing a chequebook. I then beetled home and asked Mark, my husband, 'How do you balance a chequebook?' I can report that some things don't change.

I loved working on this gem; it was the ultimate lifestyle magazine, featuring everything coastal from beauty and fashion to food, features and travel, and boy did we get around. For the launch, the preparation for which involved blood, sweat and tears, Michael somehow managed to organise a branded Qantas jet to fly the launchgoers to Coolum Beach in Queensland. Sadly, that magazine is no longer around; it was a casualty of the challenging magazine landscape of the early 2000s. I was always keen to pimp out my two sons, Harrison and Jonah, who were nine and seven, and they even appeared on the cover of one issue. Shocking nepotism, I know, but who cares: I was the editor and it was a pretty cute cover.

Two years after the launch of *Coastal Style*, I was approached by Alison Veness, the editor of *Harper's Bazaar*, who offered me the role of beauty director/executive editor: I do love a title. It was time for me to return to my ultimate love, beauty. *Harper's Bazaar* was an amazing place to work. Alison had boundless energy and intense creativity. Our production and planning meetings were always high octane and Alison really pushed the envelope.

Australian Fashion Week had begun and we hosted the famous and fabulous Bar Bazaar: a pit stop for weary fashion goers. We also had a series of guest editors for fashion week, including Cate Blanchett and Elle Macpherson. Again, the cast and crew on this magazine were fabulous; the indefatigable mistress of magazines and all things wondrous, Pat Ingram, was our publisher and is now my boss at Fairfax Media.

On my first day at *Harper's Bazaar*, Alison asked me to produce a 64-page beauty booklet in addition to the usual 20 beauty pages in the magazine. We were off and racing. It was hard not to let the cache that went with working at *Vogue* and then *Harper's Bazaar* go to your head.

I had three years on *Harper's Bazaar*, with amazing adventures along the way. I remember an accidental meeting that I ended up having with Pat while we were both having a manicure. She talked about the possibility of ACP Magazines launching a new title and whether I might be open to a change? Pat was working behind the scenes with the launch editor Paula Joye on the concept for a new magazine to take on the power player *Marie Claire*. As they figured it, each magazine in the marketplace had an opposing player – all except for *Marie Claire* – and this left the category wide open for a newcomer.

Pat and Paula were putting feelers out to top-tier people, sounding out their interest in coming to work on a brand-spanking-new title as a joint venture with Hearst Publications. Again, they pulled together a dream team. The excitement and fear were in equal parts. I met with Paula and we talked about everything, from beauty to kids to life lessons. I loved my position at *Bazaar* but could not refuse the offer to work on what would become known as *Madison*. A floor on level 11 was assigned to us and, yet again, I had prime real estate: an office with an incredible view over St Mary's Cathedral and out over the Sydney Heads.

The launch in March 2005 with Sienna Miller on the cover was prodigious. We had officially arrived. People loved it, and feedback on the magazine from my most trusted sources, the mothers and sisters of my sons' schoolmates at Cranbrook, were thumbs up. You could cook from it, make up with it, dress by it, travel with it and get a really great read out of it. Life in the magazine industry was good.

When people find out that I work in magazines they often say it must be a bitchy environment, when in reality it is the opposite of that. I have made deep and abiding friendships and have been shown more kindness by my colleagues than anyone will ever know. The beauty pack is a close-knit posse: we travel together, eat and drink together (sometimes ten times a week at the myriad functions we attend), and we share knowledge as well as trials and tribulations. The absolute truth is that we have the best jobs in the world. I am known as Mumma in the field, which I think is a term of endearment (as well as a reflection of my venerable age).

WORKING GIRL BEAUTY

Perfecting the art of no-makeup makeup makes for a great workwear face.
If you look groomed and polished you will always have the first-impression
advantage. I never feel truly ready to face the day unless I have done my
makeup; you just never know who you might run into, so it is always a bonus
if you are looking groomed. Again, as is so often the case with beauty,
less is more. For your basic work face, make sure it is well moisturised,
and follow up with a great complexion base, whether it's tinted moisturiser,
foundation, mineral powder foundation or just concealer.

MAKEUP ARSENAL

- Start with a liquid foundation to create the perfect base;
  try **Chanel Vitalumière Fluid Makeup**.
- For a creamy concealer palette that can be mixed to suit all skin tones,
  try **Bobbi Brown Face Touch-up Palette**.
- For an instant touch of colour, try a water-resistant cheek and
  lip tint like **Becca Beach Tint**.
- Lip salves like **Lanolips Lemonaid lip gloss** or **La Mer Lipgloss**
  (a favourite of son number one, Harrison) keep lips hydrated
  throughout the day.
- Use **Chanel Blotting Paper** to mop up any excess oil. The packaging
  of these is so chic it seems a shame to actually use them but they
  really do the job.
- For an essential workday brown, taupe or chamois eyeshadow,
  try **Bobbi Brown** or **M.A.C.**
- For black or brown mascara, try **Lancôme, Kevyn Aucoin, Estée Lauder,
  L'Oréal Paris, YSL, Maybelline, M.A.C, Dior, Clinique** – the list goes
  on and on. I have succumbed to the joys of expertly applied lash

extensions and visit Love Those Lashes every two weeks for in-fills.
I have been doing this for absolutely ages and am addicted. Waking up
in the morning is no longer frightening as my lashes are defined and
done. It also means that many days I go eyeshadowless, sometimes just
applying a swipe of black kohl on the inner rim of my eyes for added
definition. This leaves the way open for experimenting with lipstick,
with myriad nudes and the occasional red for a blast of colour.

- Finding the perfect nude lipstick is my lifelong obsession, as my beauty
cohort Sherine Youssef will attest. It became a standing joke whenever
lipsticks arrive in the *Madison* office. Sherine will invariably pull out
the new nude shades and have me salivating, tempted to disloyally
overthrow my current favourites. Nude covers a range of different
hues, from natural lip-coloured shades to rose, putty, lilac, brown,
beige, dusty pink, cream . . . and from satin to matte to gloss, the range
is endless. Maybelline did an entire collection dedicated to the nude lip,
which meant even more choice for my frazzled brain. Long-standing
survivors in my kit include **Bobbi Brown** in Pale Pink, **M.A.C** in Cup and
Twig, **Kardashian Beauty En-Joystick Lip Lacquer** in Modern Mauve.
There was even a Chanel lipstick called **Darling** (a perfect apricot nude
that I convinced my boys was named after me). The beauty of nude
lipstick in all its guises is that it goes with everything and suits almost
everyone. Over the years I have blended my own nudes, sometimes
mixing lip pencil and two nude shades to get my favourite colour.

- Red power lipstick for break-out moments. The skin palette needs to
be picture-perfect to carry this off, so first get your foundation flawless.
Next, coat lashes with two coats of inky black mascara and highlight
with a pinky powder blush like **Nars Orgasm**. Lips can then play the

starring role. Line lips with matching lip liner and lipstick. My favourite at the moment is **Lady Dangerfield**. Fill in the entire lip with matching pencil and then apply lipstick with a brush for precision. Blot and then reapply. With blotting, place the tissue between your lips and kiss it. To keep the fiery red pigment away from your teeth, put your clean index finger into your mouth, close your lips around it and pull it out to sweep up any stray colour. I won't lie to you; red lips are high maintenance and need fairly constant topping up.

- Ensure your brows are well shaped, as they are the coathangers for your face. They open up your eye area and frame your face; neglect them at your peril. Start by having them professionally done, or if they are meek and mild, try brow tattooing. My brows are very fair and I went to Amy Jean Couture to have them beefed up. The tattoo lasts for about a year and I found they really framed my face. Someone even asked me if I had had a facelift when I first had them done. 'No; do I need one?' I asked. To keep brows looking polished, try a tinted brow gel. **Dior** does a fabulous one called **Diorshow Brow Styler Gel**. Always remember to brush brows up. To keep any strays at bay, invest in a good pair of tweezers such as those made by **Rubis**, and always pluck from below, not above. And remember, with brows, more is more. However, if you have butchered them to pencil thinness, there is hope. A brow growth serum like **Talika** can help reconstitute them with dedicated nightly use.
- Polished nails are a passion of mine. When I was beauty director at *Vogue*, my manicures at the nail mecca Smyth & Fitzgerald in Double Bay were a weekly highlight. Christina Fitzgerald was and is an exacting genius, the best of the best. My all-time favourite colours include **Chanel Vamp, OPI Lincoln Park** and **Essie Sand Tropez.** And my

latest favourite find, from the equally fabulous Jocelyn Petroni, is the long-lasting **Vinylux** polish in shades of white and navy. This genius product lasts around seven days and comes off with regular nail polish remover. I'm sold. For any nail removal emergencies at work, go for a dipping nail polish remover like **Sally Hansen**'s. Apart from removing polish it has an oddly satisfying feel dipping fingers into the spongy squishiness soaked in nail polish remover. An emery board stashed in every conceivable spot: bedside, glove box and desk-side, is also an essential emergency tool.

AFTER HOURS

- In your 20s, as long as your base looks flawless you can get away with outlandish experimentation – richly pigmented eyeshadows, a smattering of deftly placed glitter, gilt lipstick (I love **Tom Ford**'s gold version, placed in the centre of the lips as a highlighter over the favourite nude of the moment), pastel hair chalk, like **Kevin.Murphy Color.Bug** that can be rubbed onto hair to give a pretty shot of colour that washes out instantly. This is the time to embrace new trends and borrow from the catwalk. Post-20s, perhaps ease back on the glitter, but keep the smoky eye to the fore. Use a kohl in brown, black, purple, grey, olive or aubergine to create a soft, smudgy hint of colour under your eyes or go for complete panda rings. Experimenting with colour is fun. The golden rule remains, though: never go to bed without taking all your makeup off, as it can block pores and trap oil, leading to bacteria build-up and blemishes. If you have lost the will to cleanse your makeup off after a long night, resort to makeup-removing wipes; my favourites are **Neutrogena**.

WORKING IT

DESKSIDE MUST-HAVES

Having three beauty kits stashed in my handbag, at my desk and in the glovebox has saved me in many beauty emergencies when I have been caught on the run. These consist of:

- A mini-can of **Klorane Dry Oat Milk Shampoo** is a desert island essential, as it va-va-vooms hair in an instant. Tip your head upside-down, spray it on the roots, then give it a quick tousle. It creates great volume and texture.
- A mini-can of lightweight hairspray fixes flyaway hair.
- A fat eye pencil such as those made by **Charlotte Tilbury** and **Clinique** are great options for an instant smoky eye to take you from deskside to barside. Just line the upper and lower lid with a sweep of colour and you are ready to go.
- For me, my trusty **Shiseido Liquid Compact foundation** is a don't-leave-home-without. I discovered this gem in my early days at *Vogue* and it has been a staple ever since. My skin is on the oily side, so I invariably need a top-up mid-afternoon. With this little beauty, my foundation coverage is complete in a matter of moments.
- Lipstick is also non-negotiable: wherever I am, I can't be without the ultimate no-mirror lipstick: **Clinique Black Honey**. One slick of this incredibly easy-to-apply, berry-coloured lipstick tint is all it takes to wake up my lips. For nude lipstick on the go, I am currently running with the universally flattering **M.A.C Twig**.
- A makeup touch-up stick like **Revlon**'s can quickly de-smudge any mascara fallout or ill-placed eyeshadow.

- Never underestimate the power of freshly brushed hair. My favourite beast, which travels with me everywhere, is the **Mason Pearson baby Nylon & Bristle hairbrush**. I have the cream version but it also comes in baby blue.

- **Dior**'s cuticle cream has serious desktop appeal. Keep it handy for some much-needed cuticle love. Combine this with a good SPF hand cream; **Clarins** do a good one. Out of sight means out of mind, so be sure to keep these two in view.

- I never feel quite complete unless I am wearing fragrance. Mini rollerball versions mean you can have multiples on the go. Four I am flirting with at the moment are **Kai Perfume Oil**, with a single intoxicating note of white gardenia; **Byredo Parfums Roll-on-Oil** in Tulipe, a mix of delicate florals and fresh green stems; **Diptyque Eau Rose Roll-On**, rose at its best, piqued by notes of musk and lychee; and a stash of **Kiehl's Oil Portable** in Musk Essence, a musky unisex fragrance and coriander. In fact, if I could have every one of the Kiehl's rollerballs to go I would be in scent heaven.

WORKING
IT

2

TRIPPING
AROUND
THE
WORLD

MY TRAVELS AS A BEAUTY JOURNALIST over the years have been extensive, and I invariably get the prize for the journalist who has flown the furthest. For some launches, I've even spent more time in the air than on the ground. The first trip I ever took was in my role as beauty editor at *Mode*, when I went with Louis Vuitton and Moët Hennessy to Bangkok for the launch of Guerlain's Samsara, a rich, woody, floral, oriental scent that was created by Jean-Paul Guerlain in 1989. We flew first class and tried not to look like novices as we grappled with the fancy seat dials. The highlight was the splendid candlelit dinner for a hundred, held for the world beauty media at the Oriental Hotel. This was a serious pinch-me moment, and I can still recall vividly the intoxicating Samsara scent combined with the headiness of the Bangkok night air.

And so began the series of incredible journeys I've taken for beauty. The fragrance trail has included Florence, for the launch of Ferragamo's very first perfume, Salvatore Ferragamo pour Femme, created by Jacques Cavallier in 1998, when I was working at *Vogue*. I was so massively jet-lagged that, as I had arrived on the morning of the event, which was held in the evening, I started to hallucinate over dinner. You know the feeling – when you start to slide into a parallel universe? I made it to the end of the night, but only just; however, I did manage to absorb the new fruity/floral scent, a delightful heady blend of apricot, rose, musk and almond.

TRIPPING
AROUND
THE WORLD

This was only the beginning of the three eventful days that lay ahead: our hosts had planned several excursions for us, including a dinner with the Ferragamo family at Leonardo and Maria Beatrice Ferragamo's family villa in the hills of Florence. A winding cypress-lined drive delivered us up to the beautiful villa, where the family was so warm and welcoming, it felt more like a dinner party than a fragrance launch. We sat in a room decorated with the most breathtaking eighteenth-century frescoes and ate a delicious Tuscan dinner. The night floated on and it felt as if we were in a movie. The following day, the special treatment continued as we were granted access to the secret Corridoio Vasariano, an enclosed, raised passageway that connects the Uffizi Gallery to the Pitti Palace and houses some rarely seen Renaissance artwork, including a number of self-portraits by Filippo Lippi, Rembrandt and Velázquez. The passageway was designed to allow the Medici to walk secretly and safely from the Palazzo Vecchio to the Pitti Palace, where they lived. I remember peeking out of one of the porthole windows and looking down at the crowds milling on the Ponte Vecchio below. I have always loved Florence and this experience only deepened my affection for it. Those were three incredible days; time slowed down and I was able to savour Florence in all its glory.

*F*ROM FLORENCE I TRAVELLED TO PARIS for meetings and the beginning of my test-drive career. I ended up having four facials over three days. Even for me, that was serious overload. It all began at the home of the luxury L'Institut Guerlain on the Champs-Élysées and

I was quite nervous: all that history and beauty power. There was lots of steam and many blackhead extractions, followed by a luxurious facial. My first facial in Paris – tick. The following day, I headed into a department store and had a Clarins facial while gazing up at a frescoed ceiling. My skin was analysed and the therapist targeted hydration, a longstanding concern of mine. I have oily skin but suffer from dehydration, which doesn't seem fair, really. Feeling taut and terrific, but probably at my limit where facials were concerned, I still had two facials scheduled for the next day – I'm always on the prowl for the next beauty instalment. Either facial in isolation would have been fantastic, but my skin had gone on strike, overloaded with a little too much loving attention. As I staggered in for facial number four, my facialist clocked my sensory overload and brought out her secret weapon: chilled crystal balls, which she rolled across my cheeks to calm and soothe my skin.

To say this trip to Paris was jam-packed is an understatement; looking back, there was not a moment to spare. While I was there, I also interviewed the legendary, very talented fragrance maker Annick Goutal, in her private perfume studio, situated at the base of her beautiful house in St-Germain-des-Prés. I was completely starstruck as I sat with this incredible woman, surrounded by everything that inspired her, flacons and testers as far as the eye could see. I was already a devotee of Annick Goutal Eau d'Hadrien (a fresh, grassy unisex scent that is much loved by the fashion set) and Gardenia Passion, based on the scent of gardenias after a rain shower, surrounded by jasmine, tuberose and orange blossom. In our interview, she also introduced me to Petite Cherie, a fragrance that she created as a gift for her daughter Camille, a fruity floral fragrance with notes of peach, pear, rose and musk.

TRIPPING
AROUND
THE WORLD

We talked of her early years working in her father's chocolate shop in Aix-en-Provence, where she would spend hours tying ribbons around little chocolate parcels; her life as a pianist and model in London; and how she returned to Paris to work with a friend, selling Swiss face creams. She repackaged and re-scented the creams in be-ribboned pouches, which she sold from home, and from there she went on to create her mind-blowing scents based around all things meaningful to her, such as favourite holiday spots and family. She ended up opening her first Annick Goutal boutique, all golden and inviting, on rue de Bellechasse in the Seventh Arrondissement in December 1980.

This was a truly pivotal moment in my career. I was, as it turned out, the last journalist to interview her before she died in 1999 after a long battle with cancer, leaving a legacy of 20 unique fragrances to her name.

Thinking about this initial trip, when I had just started my role at *Vogue* as beauty director, always brings back a lot of emotions for me, and it set the mood for so many amazing experiences that were to come – and still keep coming.

On a later trip to Paris, we spilled out at Charles de Gaulle airport just as some seriously intense late-autumn weather was starting; the snowflakes were as big as golf balls. In fact, later in the week, the snow was so deep the government closed down the city. We were there with the lovelies from L'Oréal Paris, staying at the supremely chic, centrally located Sofitel Hotel. We ventured out into the −4 °C night and onto rue Saint-Honoré, my favourite shopping street ever: Christian Louboutin (twinkling shoes beckon); YSL, the Lanvin and Hermès windows . . . With jet lag looming, a pit stop at the plush red-and-gold festooned bar at the Hôtel Crillon was essential: a glass of sancerre, which became our drink for the trip, and scrumptious cheese.

On this trip I visited the École Nationale Supérieure des Beaux-Arts, which is never open to the public; you've got to admire the pulling power of cosmetic giantess L'Oréal Paris. It was here we were introduced to the upcoming cosmetics ranges to be launched in the next six months. My favourite lipstick from this trip was, of course, the L'Oréal Paris nude shade, Colour Riche Made For Me Intense in Sepia/Silk, while the favourite foundation was L'Oréal Paris Infallible Foundation Brush, a genius all-in-one foundation with built-in brush.

I have too many favourite spots in Paris to mention them all, but some of the highlights include Café de Flore on the corner of Boulevard Saint-Germain and rue Saint-Benoît. This café is famous for its A-list clientele and we had our own rubber-necking moment as the fabulously chic aristocrat and beauty Inès de la Fressange wafted by, and I also spotted actor Owen Wilson. At Les Deux Magots, I recommend the delicious syrupy hot chocolate. Hôtel Costes is a must, with its all-black lacquered paintwork, jewel-coloured roses and the distinctive, eponymous fragrance permeating the halls. Great spot for a martini – try for a table in the internal courtyard. The Market is a great place to have dinner, all beige banquettes with soft wooden accents. The Cristal Room, Galerie-Musée Baccarat, is in a former private mansion with marble pillars, sky frescoes and magnificent chandeliers. It is so OTT that you half expect Louis XIV to come flouncing in. I had a lucky escape here – we had finished a sumptuous dinner and as we were leaving the building, I almost catapulted down the magnificent marble staircase. My stiletto heel caught the edge of the step and I was

*TRIPPING
AROUND
THE WORLD*

left hanging by my fingernails on the balustrade. Café du Marche des Enfants Rouge is a cute bistro with the best tarte tatin ever.

As always, I came home from this trip with a pair of souvenir shoes – er, in fact, two pairs as I recall: a pair of thigh-high Sergio Rossi boots with a gold chain ankle detail that I still march out in proudly, and a pair of black Christian Louboutin toe-cleavage pumps, also still very much in service. To date, I have collected a pair of pink Christian Louboutin Mary Janes; caramel ankle boots from Etro, multiple pairs of YSL sandals and a pair of Prada loafers with chain detail from my Paris beauty excursions.

*M*Y LAST TRIP AS BEAUTY DIRECTOR for *Madison* was yes, you guessed it, to Paris, where the luscious French hair care brand Kérastase was launching the styling arm of its range early in 2013. Kate Moss was the face and Luigi Murenu the guest stylist; my favourite product from that launch turned out to be Spray à Porter, a styling product that creates perfectly tousled, beach-inspired hair. Of all my trips, this was the most whirlwind. Fly in at 3 p.m.; fly out a day and a half later at 9 p.m. After checking in to the Westin on rue de Castiglione – perfect location – I hit the ground running.

To combat jet lag, my first stop was the Carita Spa at 11 rue du Faubourg Saint-Honoré for an emergency facial. It happened to be Valentine's Day and my kind host and I found ourselves dining with a posse of couples out celebrating. He told me that 'V-Day' is huge in France – who would have thought? From a Valentine's Day dinner to the launch the next day, then a spot of shopping before hopping on the flight back to Sydney – blink and you'd miss it.

O

N MY TRAVELS TO FRANCE FOR WORK, I've even made it down to the south of France, where I visited the famous Avène les Bains therapeutic spa. The first stop was Toulouse and a degustation dinner at La Corde: I remember seven wines for seven courses, foie gras (a specialty of the region), scallops in blueberry vinegar, asparagus and crème fraîche, soup, and truffles at every turn. I was there as a guest of the company Pierre Fabre, a vast French empire of pharmacy-based products with a cult following around the world. Brands such as Avène (skin care designed for sensitive skin and loved by dermatologists, me and pretty much everyone I know), Klorane (hair care with THE best dry shampoo), Galenic, Elancyl (for cellulite) and René Furterer (fab high-end hair care).

The supreme highlight was staying in Monsieur Pierre Fabre's 1875 chateau, Domaine du Carla in Castres. I had dinner in the family dining room and partook of the world-famous cheese trolley, which is wheeled around the room, groaning with 21 cheeses from the local region. We were there on 1 June 2008, when Yves Saint Laurent sadly died in Paris. I remember coming down the stairs to be met with the news, splashed over the front page of *Le Monde*, that he had died of brain cancer. The world was in mourning, as were we. He was one of the greatest designers ever. According to his partner Bergé, they decided not tell Saint Laurent of his terminal condition. Bergé said, 'I have the belief that Yves would not have been strong enough to accept that.'

TRIPPING
AROUND
THE WORLD

His ashes were scattered in his beloved garden in Marrakech in Morocco. We went on to discover more about Avène, but the news stayed with me for the rest of the trip.

After leaving the sanctuary of the castle, our next stop was the historic Avène Dermatological Hydrotherapy Centre, which is attached to the Hôtel Val d'Orb, Avène les Bains. The plumbing in this mountain retreat reaches directly into the healing spring waters, which work their way up from 800 metres underground through the subsoil of the Cévennes Mountains and in the process become a finely balanced blend of minerals, trace elements and silicates with anti-inflammatory properties. Avène water is used to treat everything from skin conditions to rheumatism and chest infections.

It all began in 1743 when the Marquis de Rocozels had a horse with eczema, which was cured by drinking and swimming in the Avène spring water. In 1990 the Avène brand was born, packaging its products under medical-grade conditions. The centre is run by dermatologists, offering a program of four daily treatment sessions over three weeks. The treatments include a 20-minute hydrotherapy bath followed by a shower, as well as drinking one-and-a-half litres of the spring water each day.

I was lucky enough to have a treatment, although I had to suppress a slight phobia of catching a skin disease as I hopped into the bubbling spring-water bath. The water is tepid (25.6 °C – too hot and skin conditions can be irritated) and quite relaxing. From here, I was escorted to the shower, where you have 10 minutes of

We were there when Yves Saint Laurent sadly died in Paris. I remember coming down the stairs to be met with the news … The world was in mourning, as were we.

showering followed by 10 minutes under a fine mist. This experience was a little on the chilly side, but my skin did feel incredibly soft and supple afterwards.

But the trip for which I received the prize (in a speech no less) for travelling the furthest, was to Monte Carlo the home of holistic skin care brand Biotherm. Just getting there I clocked up 32 hours of travel time, spending more time in the sky than on the ground. I flew to Hong Kong first, then Zurich, Paris and finally on to Nice. From there, I was driven to the tiny principality of Monaco. Monte Carlo itself occupies a mere 2.02 square kilometres. We shot through the narrow streets that host the grand prix every year and arrived at the Monte Carlo Bay Hotel. My room had views of the aquamarine ocean and pink-tinged cliffs — all sun-drenched and giving the impression of opulence, reflected in the hotel's clientele. Ricky Martin was staying on a locked floor directly above mine — so near, yet so far.

The invitee list for this launch consisted of 84 journalists from every part of the globe, and moi. Monte Carlo is its own wealthy micro-cosm: outside the Hôtel de Paris was a string of Lamborghinis. This town is extreme in every respect: sport, fashion, sailing, beauty. I gazed with awe at the exquisite Lanvin store, YSL, Chloe, Dior, Gucci . . . so much to buy, so little to spend. I remember my greatest financial achievement: spending ONLY eight euros on lunch.

The bijou centre of Monte Carlo is perfectly proportioned, centring around Place Du Casino and Avenue Des Spélugues, and the marina is always choked with the most OTT yachts (private cruise liners, really) you will ever see gathered in one spot. My favourite-from-afar was named *Miss Money Penny*.

TRIPPING
AROUND
THE WORLD

The Biotherm 'experience' party was at Key Largo Villa (apparently Bill Clinton came to stay the following day). We were whisked over to the other side of Monte Carlo, where parked outside the villa we saw the owners' runabout, a 30-berth cruiser; the villa itself is perched on top of a cliff, about as close to the sea as you can get without falling in. Lush white lilies and strategically placed fairy lights surrounded a beautiful pool, around which Biotherm dignitaries and stylish mag types mingled. Needless to say, I knew absolutely no one, but was swiftly adopted by the Italian *Vogue* contingent.

From Lucien Aubert, who is the director of the Biotherm Research Laboratory, I learnt all about pure thermal plankton, which is found in the mountain spa water and is the cornerstone of the brand. Apparently the soldiers of ancient Rome bathed in the mountain spring water to help heal their battle injuries, and originally the thermal plankton was laboriously collected on planks of wood until, in 1994, the Biotherm biologists discovered how to reproduce it using bio-fermentation. Got to love scientific breakthroughs. The hero of the Hydra-Detox range is the Detoxifying Moisturizing Cream that became my moisturising staple on that trip. I got to dine with Lucien Aubert at La Mandarine restaurant at the Port Palace hotel. Overlooking the marina that night we got philosophical, reflecting on the fact that no matter how big your yacht is, someone else is guaranteed to have something bigger.

Hot spots in Monte Carlo included Zebra restaurant, Bar and Bouef right next door to Jimmy'z nightclub, and The Beach Club, where the royal family swims. I ran into a friend who was staying there so we hung out by the pool and people-watched.

C<small>LOSER TO HOME, IN AUSTRALIA,</small> the excursions have been wondrous too, such as the time I went to Uluru with L'Oréal Paris for the launch of Dermo-Expertise UV Perfect. I am passionate about sunscreen and its anti-ageing and life saving abilities, as my regular readers know. What better place to have a sun care launch than in the heart of Australia's Red Centre, with its icing-sugar-fine, ochre-red sand and blazing sun? We were in the thick of it, staying within cooee of Uluru, one of the largest 'clean skin monoliths' in the world. Uluru sits 348 metres above ground level and is 9.4 kilometres in circumference. We saw it at sunset as we dined under the stars and at sunrise – magical. I also picked up some desert lingo, such as 'It's a three-dingo morning' (ie. it's bloody freezing). According to our Uluru guide, the Aboriginal people who live in the area keep dingoes as pets, and the colder it gets, the more of them they'll cuddle up to at night.

Qualia, on Hamilton Island, has also been a hot spot for a number of amazing beauty launches. The beauty media are always spoiled; on one occasion we each had our own golf buggies, with our names emblazoned on the front, for getting around the resort and the island. Also in the mix there is usually a sleek cruiser, a helicopter, and of course, champagne.

I promise you I know how lucky I am; as I write, lots of memories come flooding back. Imagine my unbridled joy when I was offered a trip to the Whare Kea Lodge & Chalet, which has won a Relais & Châteaux award, in Wanaka on New Zealand's South Island. Now, this place is seriously magical and majestic. The scenery is breathtakingly beautiful and the lodge is in prime position, perched overlooking the glacial Lake Wanaka. The view from every single vantage point

TRIPPING
AROUND
THE WORLD

is astonishing; I think it is probably the most beautiful scenery I have ever seen.

The lodge is owned by Louise and Martyn Myer and there is also a snow chalet nestled high up in the mountains, which we visited by helicopter. Now, the rooms aren't cheap, but you do get plenty of bang for your buck – drinks, canapés, a five-course degustation dinner and à la carte breakfast. I tried a fresh sweetcorn velouté with Cloudy Bay surf clams, local saffron and chorizo, chestnut mushroom carbonara with quail egg pancetta, reggiano and smoked cream, a fresh koura (a New Zealand crayfish) taco with avocado, mango, chilli and lime, followed by sous-vide Cadrona lamb with young carrots, Jerusalem artichoke puree and lamb jus, and finally, white Valrhona chocolate and espresso semifreddo with chestnuts, fresh figs and poached pear. Every single morsel was delicious, and my favourite wine of the trip was the Seresin Estate Sauvignon Blanc 2010 from Marlborough.

There was lots to do apart from blissing out on the scenery and food. I went to Mou Waho Island, home to the shameless and flightless Buff Weka bird. This bird species was on the verge of extinction until it was introduced to the predator-free island. While we stopped for lunch, one bumbled around us amiably. I also went by chopper to the Whare Kea Chalet, perched on top of the world. The mountains were dusted with snow, glittering in the brilliant sun, and we had an awe-inspiring ride back as the helicopter flew over the glacier and through the mountain peaks.

I even flew in a Tiger Moth, very similar to the one my father-in-law learnt to fly in during the Second World War – this plane was OLD. Pilot Pete landed it on the grass runway at the back of the lodge.

I remember getting kitted out in overalls and a flying jacket. Flying in the open air was astounding and I suppressed the desire to reach back and hold Pete's hand in an *Out of Africa* moment.

*M*Y FIRST VISIT TO TOKYO was to interview Aerin Lauder, Estée Lauder's granddaughter, at the Park Hyatt. She was on the final leg of her whistlestop tour of Asia for some scouting and trend spotting, immersing herself in Japanese culture and making a number of store visits. I think her team took pity on me because I was travelling alone, as they let me tag along with them everywhere. Aerin and I zoomed around Tokyo in a black limo, flanked by lots of security, and scoped the famous shopping avenue Omotesand and the Harajuku fashion district, as well as calling in to the cool Tsumori Chisato boutique. I also attended an official lunch where Aerin presented; there was a tiny glitch in the order of the slides and one of her offsiders humorously summed it up with a phrase I would take back to Australia and run with: the snafu (situation normal, all fucked up). On that trip I felt like one of the team.

The Japanese are famous for their devotion to beauty products and love of innovation, and their eye for detail when it comes to both the product and the presentation is legendary. Double cleansing is a cult in Japan and has also taken off here. This process deals with excess sebum and makeup products in the first phase, while the second phase targets dust, bacteria, sweat and dead skin cells. Love this technique – you just need to set aside a little time. First, cleanse with a cleansing

TRIPPING
AROUND
THE WORLD

oil to get rid of sebum and makeup, then wash it off and use a cleanser to mop up the rest. Make sure to massage the product onto your face to get the best and cleanest result. Try to resist cleansing laziness; do this morning and night (I should really heed my own advice). Shiseido, SKII, Kanebo, Pola Red and Sumi Haigou are all classic examples of great Japanese cleansing lines.

My travels have also placed me in extreme conditions, which have had their own beauty challenges and rewards. The Scandinavian Baths in Whistler Canada in the dead of winter was a highlight. It was one of those crystal-clear days unique to snow country. I had been rugged up and my skin was feeling dry because of the altitude and the heating, so I headed out of town to the Scandinavian Baths while my family careened around the mountains, risking life and limb. The baths experience goes like this: you strip down to swimmers and swathe yourself in a dressing gown, ready for the self-dunking. The process is undertaken in complete silence (not my natural state) as you wend your way between the outdoor hot and cold baths dotted around the heart of a spruce and cedar forest overlooking the mountains. The changes in temperature as you dip yourself in the different baths are extreme: from hot (40 °C) to cold (17 °C). You warm the body for 10 to 15 minutes, dunk yourself in cold water for 20 to 30 seconds, and then relax for 15 minutes in a toasty sun-soaked glass-panelled room, then repeat this process three to four times. The setting and the sensation were unbeatable and my skin felt amazingly smooth afterwards. I could have stayed here for days.

*T*HE USA IS ALSO A MUCH-LOVED BEAUTY DESTINATION, and New York and LA are very much on the radar. Clinique took me to LA for the launch of its Repairwear Laser Focus, where I stayed at the swank Beverly Wilshire, right next to shopping mecca Rodeo Drive. As always before I fly, my maintenance needs to be up to date: fake tan is essential, as is a mani and pedi, a little bit of artful lasering, the all-important hair colour appointment (let's face it, you can never be too blonde in LA), and of course a repack of the travel wet pack.

It's not all fun and games, of course; I work hard when I am away. On this trip we heard from Dr Ron Moy, President Elect of the American Academy of Dermatology, who was busy alerting us to new buzzwords: dermasurgery; immunostimulators; hair cloning; super lasers for wrinkles, veins and cellulite; permanent muscle relaxers using radio frequency; permanent fillers from stem cells; the future sunscreen pill . . . This took us into the beauty tech zone, ready for our introduction to Clinique Repairwear Laser Focus. The launch itself took place in a palatial modern mansion, dotted with plush white leather sofas, with views overlooking the valley. We were informed that in your 20s, you get 'starter wrinkles', which over time develop into full-blown ones. Clinique said that to tackle wrinkling it had developed a product that would not only repair wrinkles that had already formed, but would protect against future ones.

We all raced back to the hotel in full test-drive mode, ever keen to combat wrinkles, to begin the trialling process: applying Repairwear Laser Focus in the morning with sunscreen and then again at night. Next on the schedule was a power yoga work-out (sounded a bit like a contradiction in terms to me) with celebrity yoga expert Mark Blanchard of True Power Yoga fame. He counted celebrity 'stretchies' Jennifer Lopez, Rachel Griffiths and Drew Barrymore among his clients. My fear factor was high, but Blanchard attempted to put us at ease, saying that there was no pressure and that everyone was to take it at their own pace. The words 'a challenging, heart-pounding work-out' stuck in my head, though, and I struggled balancing downward dogs with upward cats. I absolutely drew the line at doing a forward roll, which I haven't done since I was eight years old.

I updated my LA address book with the restaurant Tavern, which has divine washed-out khaki walls and an amazing skylight. I even remember what I ate: sweetcorn soup with avocado cream and cilantro (coriander); 'The Devil's Chicken' with braised leeks, onions and mustard breadcrumbs, followed by a 'Snickers bar' salted peanut caramel and vanilla ice-cream. The next night we dined at Chateau Marmont, where I spotted the actor Adrien Brody dining with some friends, while I chowed down on backstrap beef with seriously the best fries ever. Cecconi's West Hollywood with its sunlit terrace and fabulous pizzas was also cool and I found a fabulous ceramic deer head at Empiric. The Grove shopping mall – where to begin – for just about anything your heart desires. The state-of-the-art Phillip Lim store was a highlight, and Intermix has every cool designer your heart could desire. At the hotel, I had a top-drawer manicure and pedicure seated in the 'Rolls Royce' of pedicure chairs, and at the spa at the Beverly Wilshire I had a life-changing Swedish massage.

And how about this for a lucky break? I had two back-to-back trips in the US; the dovetailing couldn't have been better. The first was to New York with Elizabeth Arden, where I stayed at The W Hotel at Park Avenue South. We proceeded to eat our way around the town in between meetings: luscious velvet cupcakes from Magnolia Bakery; delicious fare at The Spice Market; then dinner at the Bergdorf Goodman restaurant on the seventh floor, which was chic chic chic. Honey wooden floors, celadon walls and astounding high-backed leather pod chairs – very tryst friendly. Amazing views of Central Park and the perfect spot for a martini; we added Napoleon Crab Pasta and a restorative glass of Veuve.

I still have dreams about Saks Fifth Avenue's shoe department, which, by the way, has its very own postcode; just think of it as the Vatican of the shoe world. We got an insight into the Elizabeth Arden Prevage Body Total Transforming Anti-aging Moisturizer, which targeted all things Australian: age spots, sun damage and pigmentation. Some of my other favourites in the stable include Ceramide Gold Ultra Lift and Strengthening Eye Capsules, and the Peel & Reveal Revitalising Treatment, which re-texturises and exfoliates with a fabulous fanned brush.

But the pièce de résistance had to be the facial at the original Red Door Salon at 691 Fifth Avenue. Behind the gigantic red door, it is all space-age curves and nail-varnish-red lacquered walls housing the Arden arsenal of beauty, complete with a sparkling vintage chandelier. I had an old-school Russian facialist called Nina who placed a hot pack on my stomach, which I still remember as it was incredibly comforting. She cleansed and extracted and this was followed by a hot and cold stone massage. I have also visited the new Red Door Salon at 663 Fifth Avenue. It is well worth booking in for a facial or blow-dry.

TRIPPING
AROUND
THE WORLD

*T*HEN FROM ARDEN IN NEW YORK IT WAS ON TO LA with Napoleon Perdis and a bevy of beauty editors for the launch of NP Set Cosmetics. One of my favourites from the launch ended up being the Taupe Eye Palette Chicago. Napoleon's deeply charming driver Peter picked me up from the airport; there was no time to change into 'glamorous' dinner wear, so I ended up channelling my boho look and dragging my luggage. I was surprised I even made it past the maître d' of the super-swanky STK in West Hollywood, who relieved me of my bag with a sniff, saying, 'We don't often store luggage here.' I was ushered to a table full of jolly journalists and our host, the irrepressible Napoleon.

Next destination, Palm Springs. We drove through the desert, which was dotted with massive windmills, and arrived at the Spanish-style Colony Palms Hotel in Canyon Drive, Palm Springs, on the edge of the Coachella Valley — lots of terracotta and cream tiles and mosaic floors, a lush pool and a pretty tented pavilion. I was lucky enough to score a Casita suite with outdoor jacuzzi. This hotel is steeped in gangster history: Al Capone used to drink here in the underground speak-easy. It was also frequented by Clark Gable, Jack Benny, the Marx Brothers, Frank Sinatra and Jack Dempsey.

There was so much to take in in Palm Springs. We had lunch and massages at Frank Sinatra's mid-century pad, and were waited on by our very own pool boy. Sinatra's house has been preserved exactly as it was when Ol' Blue Eyes lived there, right down to the crack in the bathroom basin made when, in a high temper, Frank smashed a champagne bottle into it. There are acres of shag pile, *Jetsons* furniture, a gigantic turntable, a pool shaped like a piano and loads of celebrity snapshots, including the infamous JFK, Elvis, Sammy Davis Jnr, Dean Martin, Marilyn

Monroe, Ava Gardner . . . And there we were sipping champagne; it was a pinch-yourself moment. Just call us the mouse pack.

An expedition to the gigantic Cabazon mall was not for the faint-hearted: no-one does a mall like the Americans, and we had two hours of unfettered shopping time. On offer: Burberry, Prada, Converse, YSL, Chanel, Coach, Barneys and so much more.

I OFTEN THINK OF THE MAD LITTLE ANECDOTES that are part and parcel of travelling. I was away on a trip to New Zealand to cover New Zealand Fashion Week with my friends from M.A.C Cosmetics when my delightful partner in crime Jodie Matthews reminded me of a trip to Brazil that I took when I was at *Madison*, for the launch of M.A.C Cosmetics Mineralise range. Now, there were a couple of mishaps on this trip, but then I was heading halfway around the world to the effervescent Rio de Janeiro, so I probably should have expected no less.

It all began before we even left the ground. The visa application was slightly tricky as I am so used to being spoonfed by the amazing beauty PRs who punctuate my life that I failed to realise that I required a yellow-fever vaccination. Epic fail. I didn't realise my potentially fatal error until I returned to Sydney, only to be asked for my yellow-fever certificate. My what? Customs took me aside along with a number of other fools and told us that if we developed flu-like symptoms we had to go straight to accident and emergency. Yikes. And if my eyes started to bleed, then there was no hope as yellow fever is invariably fatal. I could feel my temperature rising on the spot.

TRIPPING
AROUND
THE WORLD

The ever-inventive M.A.C team were launching their latest bedazzling colour collection, Semi-Precious, in the heartland of raw ingredients for beauty products, Brazil. The flight was quite long as you first fly to Argentina, touch down and pick up a connecting flight. I'd managed to pick up a 'travel husband', that is, an unsuspecting kind man forced to deal with my anxious-traveller idiosyncrasies. Both of us got off the flight in Buenos Aires with no idea what the transit procedure was. The ground staff didn't seem to know either. Finally someone took pity on us and guided us through the customs area, which required a money 'exchange'. We had been told our bags would be automatically loaded onto the connecting flight, but I spotted mine sitting abandoned in the middle of the airport floor. I grabbed it and we headed for the bus, which took an hour to drive us to a totally different airport for the onward journey. It might have been helpful to know this before we left Sydney. I'm just saying.

It was a long haul and we finally arrived in Rio de Janeiro to check in at the drop-dead-gorgeous Fasano Hotel designed by Philippe Starck. The staff wear Ocimar Versolato-inspired uniforms and the materials used around the hotel are Brazilian-influenced, from the Îpe flooring to the gigantic Piquiá tree stump used for the reception desk. The rest of the hotel is adorned with Grecian marble, 19th-century Argentine brickwork and Chinese onyx.

I collapsed into my beautiful room with its Rodrigues furnishings, ear-shaped mirrors and balcony overlooking the sea. Don't you just love that feeling when you strip off the dusty flight clothes, shower, robe up and immediately order room service? The hotel porter arrived with my meal and then lo and behold propositioned me. I politely rebuffed him and immediately called my PR minder, who had flown in from New York, to laugh about this ludicrous encounter, only to discover that the same guy had tried this line on her too. Obviously he targets all incoming female guests.

I remember waking up to a brilliant blue day and heading up to the rooftop pool, a haven with a panoramic vista up and down the beachfront of Ipanema Beach, abutted by awe-inspiring mountains, all under the watchful gaze of the Art Deco statue of Christ the Redeemer, perched 710 metres above sea level – incredible. To get us in the mood we headed downtown with our trusty driver to sample some Brazilian fashion spots. Two highlights: Mixed, where I bought a pair of navy flares, and shoe haven Schutz, where I picked up a hot little pair of leopard pumps for a song. Later that night, we dined at landmark restaurant Antiquarius, where we ate delicious Portuguese-inspired food, surrounded by whitewashed walls and exposed beams painted paprika red.

Every day of that trip was sun-drenched and our visit to Floresta da Tijuca for an Amazon rainforest hike was no exception. We even had bodyguards who flanked us the entire time as safety was a high priority. I was thinking 'woman versus the wild', so I had the hiking gear at the ready, but some of our colleagues had interpreted the instructions differently, turning up in Chanel ballet flats and Louis Vuitton totes. The rainforest was thick, punctuated with waterfalls and extremely humid; it was also infested with mosquitoes, which are potential yellow-fever carriers – little did I know the danger I might have been in. Back to the hotel for more rooftop gazing before the official drinks party, where pretty much everyone was dressed in M.A.C black. Crowd favourite, Caribbean makeup god and M.A.C senior vice-president of makeup

artistry, Gordon Espinet, held court and gave us a taste of what was to come at the official launch. Gordon is legendary for his makeup skills and deep-seated charm.

The city's Museum of Modern Art was the venue for the launch of the much-anticipated Semi-Precious makeup collection. We were introduced to charismatic trendsetter and M.A.C's senior vice-president of global product development, Jennifer Balbier – believe me, she can even make the ingredients list for a lipstick sound thrilling. Her dedication to the craft of choosing colour is legendary; in fact, she painted 24 different swatches of beige on her wall in Bridgehampton so she could decide which ones looked best in daylight, dusk and evening.

The M.A.C people are nothing less than devotional about their brand and have the rules of beauty down pat. Nothing is left to chance, as you can see in each meticulously thought-out campaign. 'M.A.C,' said Jennifer, 'has had a lust for Brazil for the last nine years and today a lot of the elements of the diversity of the culture of M.A.C and the diversity of Brazil are coming together in the reinvention of the mineral makeup category. M.A.C is about trying to take some authenticity from a country, interpret it and have it be applicable to the entire world of beauty. Brazil is known for its gemstones but I think I have developed a way to absolutely use them in cosmetics.'

So how do they take the pulverised gemstones and mix them with the rich pigments to get the end product? 'We knew the minerals were going to be hot, we had no idea they were going to be that hot,' Jennifer told us. So the story unfolds: the renowned Italian baker Marco Rusto met Jennifer at a Las Vegas trade show and she asked him if he could bake minerals. His response was, 'We can bake anything.'

We were then treated to a live demonstration of how each mineralised shadow is lovingly baked to create these unique products. Each one is entirely individual because it is blended by hand.

The four magical gems that make up the base of the latest collection of 12 eyeshadows, four skin finishes and three blushes are: bronzite, reputedly good for self esteem; black tourmaline, the regulating stone, gold pyrite, good for negativity and lilac lepidolite, the peace stone. We all rushed the lacquered boxes that contained these jewel-like shadows, eager to try them. 'By folding in these four beautiful bijoux, along with the blend of seventy-seven minerals, we have created what we believe to be the most amazing mineral collection that will give the most incredible highlighting effects to the skin,' said Jennifer.

The minerals add a special degree of clarity and were adored by the 150 makeup artists (including Val Garland and Charlotte Tilbury) who test-drove them at the Ready to Wear shows. 'You know, when we showed the makeup artists the mineralised eye shadows, they always grabbed them first,' said Gordon Espinet. 'Particularly Gold Gaze. It looks almost a black gold and when you wear it you get this intense gold leaf on your eyelid. And the best thing? The mineral eyeshadows stay on like a powder and apply like a cream, so they're the best of both worlds.' This is a keeper.

AND FOR A COMPLETE CHANGE OF PACE, on one occasion I visited Procter & Gamble HQ in Cincinnati, Ohio, to get a taste of what was next from its brand Olay. The science behind the beauty

*TRIPPING
AROUND
THE WORLD*

products that enhance our looks is very serious business, and Olay's anti-ageing skin care line, Olay Professional Pro-X, is no exception.

From a whirlwind tour and rounds of interviews with the boffins, I picked up a few new buzzwords and brushed up on some others. P&G is an $80 billion company that creates hair care, pet care, deodorant, men's grooming, skincare, cleaning products, fragrances – you name it, they do it. Clairol, Covergirl, Max Factor, Pantene, Wella, SK-II, Duracell, Oral-B, Pringles, Gillette . . . to name just a few.

The buzzword at the time was genomics: this is the study of how genes function, interact with one another and respond to environmental stimuli. All of these influence how we age, and there are two main factors that determine this: intrinsic ageing and photo-ageing. The genome project identified three major contributors to the ageing of the skin: lack of hydration (700 genes affect water content in the skin), loss of collagen (40 genes have an impact on this) and inflammation (400 genes are involved).

To target the ageing process, retinoids (derived from vitamin A) are used as a chemical exfoliant, which is said to have a positive effect on the production of collagen, helping reverse some of the damage the sun does and reducing wrinkles. This is an essential part of any night-time anti-ageing skincare regime. When using vitamin A derivatives it is always essential to apply sunscreen daily, as they can make your skin more sensitive to the sun. But hey, you are doing that anyway, right?

Niacinamide can also be applied topically to improve texture, fine lines and the skin's barrier function. It is also commonly known to reduce redness and pore size, while Pal-KTTKS (a small molecule made up of five amino acids) is said to stimulate collagen synthesis and help reduce wrinkles; and Pal-KT (a peptide) is said to increase the production of collagen and help in wound healing.

On this trip I also met Dr Maritza Perez in downtown Danbury. P&G had tracked her down to work with their think tank of immunologists, surgeons and dermatologists to help create the Olay Professional Pro-X range. Her favourite product was the Hydra Firming Cream, while mine was the Age Repair Lotion, because it shields from the sun and hydrates. Marita's best anti-ageing advice: 'Use retinoids (Vitamin A) for repair of your skin, sunblock with broad spectrum ingredients and moisturisation with barrier protection. Then, if you want something a little more profound, I think everyone needs Botox as maintenance to prevent wrinkling, supplemented with facial fillers to add volume to the skin, and the third line of attack would be lasers.' A woman after my own heart – she had all the bases covered.

Getting some insight into what goes into creating an effective skincare range was a revelation of this trip. I met the genomics guru Jay Tiesman, who nailed it when he said: 'You want to make sure you are providing people with something that really works, but people need to be able to tolerate it. Basically, you're trying to find the balance between efficacy and tolerance.'

WHAT TO PACK

I always keep my travel kit packed and ready to go. But once a year I do give the kit an overhaul and stock up with fresh items. I always find this cathartic. Ziplock bags are the key to a happy life. Section out your categories, such as teeth, fragrance, skincare, makeup and medication, and have a ziplock bag for each that you store in your wet pack. This will localise and seal in any unfortunate leaks, too.

I have found that there are so many good mini versions of almost everything out there that there is no need to decant products. I did try it once and due to impatience, made a hell of a mess. Grown Alchemist Travel Kit has seven smartly packaged essential items: gel face and body cleansers, shampoo and conditioner, day cream, lip balm and body cream.

In-flight, if it's a long haul, I love hydrating masks for a big boost of moisture, and I always wear a facial oil throughout the flight. Facial spritzes are my lifesaver and I keep Aesop rose petal-infused Immediate Facial Hydrosol within reach at all times. I plait my hair to keep it contained and carry hair powder to soak up excess oil, then attempt a rock-star tousle before I disembark.

KITTED OUT

Travel kits are a great way to take the guesswork out of what to pack. Try ones dedicated to skincare, hair care and body, or narrow down your favourites from the minis and create your own customised kit. Aesop's parsley seed-based London Travel Kit is one of my favourites, the refreshing mouthwash is a must for when you have birdcage mouth. With skin care, Aspect has a basic starter kit with active cleanser, vitamin C serum, AHA exfoliator and a moisturiser.

HAIR ESSENTIALS

Hair is always so central to feeling pulled together and if you are having
a good hair day, then everything else just seems to fall into place. For a complete
care cream, try Kérastase Soleil CC Crème, which protects hair from the sun
as well as repairing and moisturising it. Apply before venturing out. Sachajuan
have a great variety of mini shampoos and their sea-algae-based Hair in the Sun
is the perfect beach and poolside companion to apply before taking the plunge.
I think if you can possibly fit a regular hairdryer into your luggage it's a must,
as the hairdryers in every hotel I have ever stayed in have absolutely no grunt.
Try Parlux 385 Light. Cloud Nine do a clever product called The Micro Wand
that is great for creating texture on the go. Also, pack a mini hairspray, such as
the beloved Elnett and the most essential item of all, Klorane Extra Gentle
Dry Shampoo with Oat Milk.

MAKING SCENTS

I love the ease and lightness of fragrance rollerballs. It means you can take a
wardrobe of them with you. Here are some of my favourites: Kai Perfume Oil,
with its single intoxicating note of gardenia. Byredo Parfums Roll On Oil in
Tulipe, a mix of delicate florals and fresh green stems. Diptyque Eau Rose
Roll-On is rose at its best, piqued by notes of musk and lychee. Kiehl's Musk
Essence Oil Portable is such a sexy unisex fragrance; I also love the Coriander
version. For the boys, Dior Fahrenheit Refillable Pocket Spray is an oldie
but a goodie with its leathery, woody, ozonic notes. With notes of grapefruit,
cardamom and cinnamon, Costume National Homme is a great travelling
companion.

ABSOLUTELY ESSENTIAL SPF50+

You know the drill by now. Keep ageing sun damage at bay by applying sunscreen 30 minutes before you venture outside and keep some in your travel tote to reapply every two hours. Dermalogica Solar Defense Booster SPF50 is a nifty little product that you can add to your moisturiser. Solar D Vitamin D Friendly Sunscreen SPF50 is an Australian sunscreen that protects from damaging UVA and UVB rays while permitting a percentage of vitamin D forming wavelengths in. If, heaven forbid, you should get sunburnt, try Shiseido After Sun Intense Recovery Emulsion.

TRAVEL PALETTES

I love a palette at the best of times but particularly when travelling, as it's a one-shot that covers every base. Bobbi Brown Warm Glow Eye Palette is serious travel candy, with its crocodile-inspired packaging and every conceivable shade of eyeshadow you could want.

TOOLS TO TRAVEL BY

- **Tweezerman Mini Slant Tweezers** are an essential stray hair extractor that make on-the-go grooming a breeze. Apart from their practicality, they're also great because they come in incredibly cute pastel shades.
- The makeup fraternity is wedded to the beauty blender **Original Makeup Sponge**. I've tried many foundation applicators and this baby wins hands down. It buffs foundation to perfection and just never dies.
- An eyelash curler is also one of those tools that should never be far from your lashes. The go-to is **Shu Uemura**, the original and best.

Creating a bend in your lashes will open the eye area and make lashes look fuller even without mascara. For travelling try tinting your lashes before you go.

- For the tangled hair challenge look no further that the mini **Tangle Teezer Compact Styler**. Works like a charm on wet or dry hair without breaking it.
- For blow-drying hair into submission, you will need to pack a full-sized bristle brush like **ghd Natural Bristle Radial Brush** to add curls and volume to your heart's desire.

FLIGHT MODE

Before I clamber on board, some serious maintenance is in order. The day before I fly, I like to look the part by having an artfully applied fake tan that instantly puts me into holiday mode. To get the tan to last the distance, I always pack a few fake-tan-enhancing items, such as Clarins Radiance Plus Golden Glow Booster. This is a genius facial fake-tanning product that can be added to any moisturiser to give an instant, building glow. I apply Bobbi Brown Highlighting Powder in Bronze Glow in spots the sun would naturally catch such as the décolletage and the top of my cheekbones. Pop it over blusher to create more depth. Then I use Napoleon Perdis Whipped Dream Tan Enhancer to help lengthen the life of my fake tan and Jurlique Sun Specialist Sunless Tanner for a fake tan top-up.

A long-lasting manicure and pedicure are also de rigueur. My favourite shades are creams, putty and opaque dusty rose for fingers and for toes, jet black or bold red. CND Vinylux, OPI and Shellac are a few long-lasting polishes to try. If you have nail painting skills and like to change up your polish while you're away, try some of my favourites, including OPI. Nail Lacquer in Chillin' Like a Villain, Essie nail polish in Urban Jungle or Chanel Le Vernis in Ballerina.

On board, just put on a face mask and relax. One of my favourites for travel is SK-II Facial Treatment Mask, chock-a-block full of the wonder ingredient, Pitera. The company discovered this in the 70s when they realised the elderly workers at a sake brewery had incredibly soft hands due to having them deep in the fermentation liquid as the sake was prepared. The boffins at SK-II researched over 350 kinds of yeast before refining the strain that worked best with skin. The mask can look a bit Phantom of the Opera, but who cares, it does a sensational job of moisturising plane-weary skin.

FLYING HIGH

Don't leave home without these on-board essentials:

- **Mecca Cosmetica Brush Set**, which comes with a handy brush cleaner.
- **SK-II Signs Eye Masks** for an instant pick-me-up.
- **Dior Crème Abricot Cuticle Cream** to keep cuticles in good nick.
- **Guinot Soothing Gel For Legs**. This product is loved by flight attendants the world over for its soothing properties.
- Keep your skin hydrated with **Kosmea Mini Hydrating Rosewater Mist**.
- **Chanel Vitalumière Aqua Cream Compact** is great for touch-ups, any time anywhere, plus it just looks so good.
- **Estée Lauder Re-Nutriv Ultimate Contouring Eye Lift**, which is great for lips too.
- **Dermalogica PreCleanse Wipes** to wipe away that inflight grime.
- **Elizabeth Arden Eight Hour Cream**: skin first aid in a tube.
- **Estée Lauder Double Wear Foundation** because, as the name suggests, it goes the distance and stays put for up to 15 hours.
- The chubby stick: the perfect travel companion, doubling as a lipstick, eyeshadow and blush. **Clinique Chubby Stick** in Heaping Hazelnut is the all-time essential nude.

TRIPPING
AROUND
THE WORLD

BOYTALK

3

*M*Y TWO SONS HARRISON AND JONAH are my proudest creations and have often influenced my perceptions of beauty. I am also lucky enough to have two wonderful step-children too, Linden and Isabel, as well as a delicious step-grandson, Louis (I am his Stephie G). Their take on some of my more outlandish treatments have caused tears of hilarity. They pretty much just call it as they see it, with none of the polite holding back that most people do.

One of my earliest memories of the power a change in a hair-style can bring – and not necessarily in a good way – was when I was working at *Harper's Baẓaar* and my editor, Alison, convinced me to go out of my comfort zone for a story. I have fine, mid-length hair and a reasonable amount of it; it is fortunately bossed into shape very easily with a bit of heat protector and hairdryer heat: love my Parlux. I wear it either straight or with a bit of volume and texture, and love nothing better than having someone else wielding the equipment. A blowdry runs neck and neck with a pedicure as one of my very favourite things.

So for this story I was dispatched to a salon to have my hair temporarily curled and styled beyond recognition. The curls were of Shirley Temple proportions (read: tight), taking my hair to just below my jawline. I returned to the office to very quietly reassuring (read: polite) comments from colleagues; it was not until I got home that truth in sentencing was pronounced. Harrison, aged seven, took one look at me and started to cry, saying in a tentative voice, 'Mummy?' Even my husband refused to give me any positive feedback. No matter how young or old, men seem to hate hair changes in their womenfolk.

Harrison always gives a completely honest appraisal and this has become more pronounced as he has gotten older; there really is no-where to hide. At around about the same time as I had my flirtation with curls for an afternoon, I began on what was to become a lifelong mission of cosmetic surgery research. When I first started editing the beauty section at *Mode* magazine, I was in my 20s and swore to myself I would never have anything 'done'. What was I thinking?

I had my first bout of Botox in the early 2000s, when I was 32, with my dear friends Kaye Scott and Lisa Sullivan at The Clinic in Bondi Junction. Injection queen Lisa initially tackled my frown lines and a week later, no more frown. Botox is based on the botulinum toxin, a protein and neurotoxin produced by the bacterium *Clostridium botulinum*, which causes botulism. It is the gold standard for relaxing wrinkles as it blocks the signals between your facial nerves and superficial muscles. As I have aged, I've treated an increasing number of areas, but always with the aim of looking rested, not frozen. I have clocked up a large bank of beauty frequent-flyer points with Kaye and Lisa, who have ministered to my every anti-ageing need.

When I arrived home after that initial Botox session, for some unknown reason, I thought that young Harrison would be interested in knowing about this amazing procedure. I explained to him the intrica-cies of what was involved and how it had taken away my frown lines. A little while later, I must have raised my voice to him, and he bounced back saying that the treatment hadn't worked because I still had a frown in my voice. Out of the mouths of babes.

W HEN HARRISON WAS 14, there was a moment of skin trauma as he started to suffer from what I considered to be simply mild acne. I was like one of those doctors who refuse to acknowledge that a family member is ill. All I could see was my handsome son with a few pimples. It got to the point where he was so exercised about it that he took my credit card out of my wallet and ordered some acne-targeting Proactiv products online. I had absolutely no idea how bad he felt; it wasn't until I read my bank statement and saw the purchase that I had any inkling. I felt so bad about having dismissed his concern that I immediately went into overdrive and got him an appointment with the king of dermatology, Chris Kearney. Chris put him on a course of Roaccutane and his skin has never looked back.

Your children are always your harshest critics. I used to have a small, and I thought innocuous, mole on my nose, just above my right nostril. Both Jonah and Harrison would draw attention to this on a fairly regular basis, and in not very favourable terms. In a weak moment, I decided to visit a plastic surgeon and have it removed. I had some pretty unsightly blue stitches that looked even worse when covered with a small bandage. Timing for these things is never good, as I then flew to New York to interview and have my makeup done by the globally renowned makeup artist Bobbi Brown. She very dexterously worked around the stitches and my makeup looked flawless. This was also where

I discovered one of my all-time favourite lipsticks, Bobbi Brown Lipstick in Pale Pink, which is great on blondes. When I arrived back home I had the stitches out, but what I hadn't factored in was that where the mole once was, there is now a half-moon-shaped, oversized pore. Am I happier with this than my original mole? Who cares? It's done now.

*T*HE BOYS ARE MY MOST-TIMES WILLING GUINEA PIGS for some of my test drives of men's treatments in my beauty column for *Sunday Life*. Memorable ones have included a family-bonding treatment at Dermalogica HQ in Artarmon. The boys had their first-ever facials and I was having a post-teenage-party recovery skin-sloughing body treatment. I hasten to add it was a vast room and I was cordoned off from them, but it was endearing seeing them with their hair nets on, lying side by side while the two therapists gave them each a customised facial and bags of product to take home at the end.

Meanwhile, I had body brushing to crank up my circulation, a warming massage, and thermal stamping that involved having a fabric bag packed with seaweed, wasabi root, oatmeal and ginger massaged into my skin. At the end of this stage, the thermal stamps are opened up and the mud contents massaged in further. The final step was a body wrap and while this 'cured', my scalp was massaged. Bliss. The finishing touch: the mud is removed with steaming-hot towels and a hydrating body cream is then worked over the skin. I managed to claw back some of the strength that party central had sapped and the boys were very blissed out, with unmistakeably dewy 'facial faces'.

*F*OR YEARS I'VE BEEN THREATENING to take the boys to have a pedicure and my moment to pounce came when Jonah had returned from six months overseas on his gap year. By the look of the state of his feet he must have gone barefoot for most of that time, including camel riding in Morocco and tending great white pointers at Marine Dynamics in Gansbaai on the Western Cape of South Africa. I booked him in, kicking and screaming, for a pedicure (sans polish) at Paddington Nails. He settled in pretty quickly and soon there was a mountain of dead skin shavings. His feet have never looked so pristine.

I have been going to my favourite podiatrist, Paul Poshoglian at Poshoglian Podiatry, for more years than I can remember. He is a whiz with the corn slicing blade and also an amazing storyteller. Paul began his career tending feet with Elizabeth Arden back in the 60s and is still going strong. I visit him on a regular basis, every four weeks, and am always at my happiest propped up on the reclining podiatry chair. Paul is never judgemental about my sky-high shoes, in fact, he is often in awe, and the reason I am still tottering around in these killers is due to his legendary skills.

Like father, like son: Paul's son Martin is also a podiatrist in the practice and is a goldmine of information on the burning issue of dry feet, which seem to get more pronounced as you age. Martin's tip is to exfoliate skin with a pumice stone in the shower and then use a urea-based cream like Try NS-8 Heel Balm Complex, which penetrates the superficial layers of skin to keep toughened skin soft. Healthy feet contribute so much to general wellbeing, so even if your shoe cupboard is full of flatties, schedule a visit to a podiatrist; your feet will thank you.

As I write this, I am sitting by a cruise ship pool as I take a voyage of discovery, and looking around at some of the men's feet on display, I fall just short of gagging. What are they thinking? Even if a pedicure is out of the question, a serious up-close-and-personal with the nail clippers is essential to keep nails in check. For me, groomed nails and toenails are non-negotiable in our family.

I HEAR THAT DAUGHTERS ARE HIGH-MAINTENANCE as they get older, but sons also have their demanding ways. Harrison was bemoaning the fact that his teeth were less than arctic white and I must admit mine could have done with a top-up too, so we headed off together to the Pitt Street Dental Centre in Sydney to have a Philips Zoom WhiteSpeed treatment, which uses a heavy-duty brightening gel and LED light technology.

I'd had this treatment done before so I was wised up on what's involved. Luckily, I am one of the very rare breed that doesn't suffer from what is so charmingly referred to as 'shooters': shooting nerve pain associated with the whitening process. The treatment starts with a thorough teeth cleaning by a hygienist, who then places a dental guard in your mouth to jack it open. The treatment is broken up into four 15-minute slots, interspersed with the application of fresh gel after each dose of light.

Unfortunately, Harrison is not one of the rare breed and by the end of the treatment he was wincing with pain, saying why hadn't I warned him? The shooters continued to come in bursts for him but by the morning were pretty much gone. It's a good idea to take some painkillers an hour before you begin to help take the edge off any pain. But you can't argue with the results. His teeth and mine were around 13 shades lighter and looked really fresh. They also send you home with a whitening kit to keep teeth looking brilliant and then you return in three months for a secondary top-up treatment.

One of Harrison's friends at the gym was so impressed with his pearly whites that he said he felt compelled to race home and clean his teeth. Never underestimate the power of word of mouth. I saw this friend's mother a few weeks later and laughingly told her about this; she gasped and said her son had taken it one step further and while visiting their family dentist for a simple check-up, had signed himself up for teeth whitening, unbeknown to her, to the tune of $900. She was not amused, but his teeth did look pretty sensational.

I am always on the lookout for new and inventive presents for my boys and one that got the tick of approval was a Hawaiian massage at the Ka Huna centre in Sydney. I had organised this treatment for Jonah before he flew to London for the beginning of his gap year, after of course having test driven it for myself. This treatment is soooo good it's practically illegal, a mixture of mermaid with octopus arms and complete abandon. You need to leave modesty at the door as it is done with you in the buff. The fluidity of the therapist's movements, combined with deep breathing and mystical whale-sounding whooping is really captivating. When I picked Jonah up after he had had this treatment, he looked as if he had been astro-travelling. This made that long haul to London really quite bearable.

THE DARLING MEN'S TOP FRAGRANCES

Both Harrison and Jonah have been fragrance devotees since they were small.
I still have an image of Jonah, aged four, in his father's dressing room with
Halston Men, a delightful scent housed in the most amazing gold flacon, copying
his father's fragrance application techniques by patting it on his little face.
He has since mastered the art of fragrance as opposed to aftershave application.
Mark, however, still considers fragrance and aftershave as interchangeable.

HARRISON: MAN WITH A MISSION

He started out as junior burger wearing Tommy Hilfiger and is now the
adventurous fragrance man. He has the famous family ability to sniff out great
new fragrances almost before I have them out of the packaging. Top of the
list at the moment are Amouage Journey Man. This is a must-have just for the
bling it adds to your dressing table, let alone the swoon-worthy, spicy, woody
fragrance made up of Sichuan pepper, bergamot, cardamom, tobacco leaves
and tonka beans. Robert Piguet Baghari is a floral, oriental, unisex scent
with its powdery, aldehydic, citrus, floral and and woody accords. And the
latest stable entry, Paco Rabanne 1 Million Absolutely Gold, is pure grunt.

JONAH: THE EXPLORER

Jonah's favourite fragrance at the moment is Tom Ford Oud Wood eau de
parfum. I have also been known to sneakily spritz some too. It is an addictive
blend of oud wood, rose wood, cardamom and pepper. Can't you just imagine
how good it smells?

Also on his list of favourites is Acqua di Parma Blu Mediterraneo Mirto di
Panarea eau de toilette, which epitomises the Mediterranean and reminds
Jonah of his time in Positano, with its notes of myrtle, blackcurrant,

lemon, lilac, orange and jasmine; and Penhaligon's Lothair, which I picked up at a fragrance showing from Nick Smart who distributes some of the world's rarest fragrances through his company, *Libertine Parfumerie*.

MARK: OLD SCHOOL
(remember, he applies fragrance to his face)

The first time I met Mark, 28 years ago, he was wearing Ralph Lauren Polo Sport (and a frilly shirt and sombrero, but that's another story). To this day, it is still one of my all-time favourite male scents. There is something so hypnotic about it, and it hits an emotional chord every time I smell it.

Mark's first foray into scent was based on his father's Geo F Trumper's West Indian Extract of Limes Cologne. Geo F Trumper started out life as an old English barbershop and is now purveyor to various members of the English royal family. A visit to the store is a must, as it's all vintage glass and wood, and the staff there are very receptive. The cologne is exactly as the name suggests: extract of limes – you can just feel a gin and tonic coming on. I am constantly stealing little hits of it, as it is a perfect early-morning scent.

Terre de Hermès was a 60th birthday gift from friends and is Mark's new favourite. He gets of lots of comments on it, and he now refers to it as his 'Chanel No. 5'.

When travelling, he takes along a 30ml travel-sized Bottega Veneta Pour Homme, which has also become my travel essential.

MEN'S GROOMING NOTES

THE HAIRY QUESTION

When it comes to men's grooming and the question of how much hair is too much, there are varying schools of thought. I am a big fan of laser hair removal and had my legs, underarms and bikini done (sorry, probably too much information) over 15 years ago with miraculous results. For men, excess hair on upper arms, shoulders, buttocks, backs or testicles can be embarrassing, but that is where laser hair removal can be so brilliant. There are a few preparation tricks to getting it right though: the area in question must be cleanly shaved 24 hours before the treatment and can't be exposed to the sun until the series of ten treatments (spaced six to ten weeks apart to align with the hair's growth cycle) is completed.

The rule of thumb with laser hair removal is no fake tanning and no waxing, epilating or plucking for four weeks prior to the treatment. It works like this: the laser is absorbed by the pigment in the hair, which in turn damages the hair follicle and retards future hair growth. The one thing to remember is that laser only treats dark hair so it doesn't work on blonde, grey or red hair, unfortunately. The process feels much like a rubber band being flicked onto your skin, and I always think it's a good idea to take a couple of painkillers half an hour before the treatment to take the edge off.

I am conducting a straw poll about the fact that lots of men seem to want to be hairless, right down to their genitals, but that lots of women like their men to be haired up in the right places. Even when it comes to chest hair, the rule of thumb seems to be keeping it trimmed rather than boy-bare. Investing in a good set of beard- and body-hair trimmers is a great way to keep things under control, and maybe straw poll your nearest and dearest to see what they think.

SHAVING

There are all sorts of shaving preparations. One of my favourites for men is the pre-shave oil from Tom Ford (of course). It provides a protective barrier and helps improve the ability of the razor to glide over the skin. To get the closest shave possible, you need to open up the pores first. Shaving after or during a hot shower gives the best skin-prepping results. Next comes the shaving cream. Old school is with a lathering brush – try The Art of Shaving Brush and Shave Cream, or for something straight out of a tube, try Clinique Cream Shave. Next, dunk a sharp blade (Harrison has just discovered the joys of the Aesop shaver complete with loose blades) into a very hot sink of water, then using gentle but firm pressure, shave with the grain of the beard. For a super close shave, re-lather and shave against the beard's grain.

After shaving, rinse with cold water to close the pores and pat skin dry. Then apply a soothing balm like ClarinsMen Super Moisture Balm.

CROSS FRAGRANCING

We humans are very good at detecting, recognising and remembering smells, and olfactory memory has a sweet way of reminding us of the great pleasures in life and sometimes the pain. According to fragrance lover Max Lake, 'Fragrances can be calming or stimulating.' Lake conducted a study looking at the chemical effects of fragrance on the brain – 'If the sniffer liked the perfume, it was followed by an alpha spike in the brainwave. A really attractive perfume makes the brain fire explosively and slow to turn off.'

Wearing men's fragrances opens up a whole new category and level of scent. I am a huge fan of artfully chosen men's fragrances and am devoted to Guerlain Vetiver, which I have a bottle of myself. It is deliciously grassy and green and was created in 1959 by the master perfumer, Jean-Paul Guerlain. Every man (and woman) needs this in their fragrant life.

Some great contenders for the cross-spritzing category include: Helmut Lang, Dunhill Desire, Penhaligon's Lords, Davidoff Cool Water, Van Cleef & Arpels pour Homme, and L'eau d'Issey Pour Homme. Delving into the rich vein of men's fragrances (as if I didn't have enough female fragrances on the go) has thrown up a new list of additions: Gucci Nobile, an aromatic fougère (a perfumer's term that means 'fern-like') with sexy warm notes; Adolfo Dominguez Agua Fresca, with its forest notes of oakmoss and citrus; and Sisley Eau de Campagne, full of wild herbs and distinctive green tomato leaves.

I love the history of fragrance. There have been pivotal male fragrance moments which have influenced the creation of female scents. Guerlain's Jicky, which launched in 1889, was the first modern perfume, with its unique, complex composition featuring fresh aromatics, spicy notes and base notes of tonka bean and vanilla. This fragrance had a mixed gender ride; nobody knows for sure whether Jicky was designed for men or women. The Guerlain Company finally asked fragrance aficionado Michael Edwards to classify it as 'unisex'.

Michael Edwards has an interesting take on the way stress and social upheaval affect our fragrance choices. He thinks that during times of upheaval, women tend to opt for more assertive scents with the woody notes that are often the base of men's fragrances. I think I may be a case in point. Where's my Vetiver? Interestingly, towards the end of World War II, Rochas' Femme launched, all assertive and woody, while Miss Dior in 1947, after the war, featured distinctive fresh, sharp, green notes.

The 50s were a return to traditional, conservative, 'role model' scents. That is, until Christian Dior's emblematic classic Sauvage for Men came into view in 1966 with its invigorating lemony freshness. Just over half the devotees were women and this, in turn, prompted the launch of sister fragrance Diorella in 1972. The latest incarnation, Eau Sauvage, is presently being fought over by my whole family.

In the 1990s the growing trend towards androgyny and the rise of unisex scents, such as Demeter's Laundromat and Calvin Klein's CK One epitomised this decade, with its clean, clear, watery notes. All I can say is keep experimenting: men can wear women's fragrances and vice versa. If you like the way it smells, dab it on. Remember, perfume is emotional sex. As nose Jean-Paul Guerlain says, 'It's men and it's women and it's the language of the dark.'

THANK GOD I HAD THAT NOSE JOB

*T*HE FIRST TIME I REALLY THOUGHT ABOUT OWNING A FRAGRANCE was at the age of 11. My brother and I were visiting my father, who was going to Europe on business, and he asked me if I wanted him to bring me back something. The fact that he had even asked this question was pretty revolutionary, so I quickly asked if he could bring me some 'channel perfume'. He laughed derisively and then corrected my pronunciation. I was mortified but it was worth the humiliation when he turned up with a bottle of Chanel No. 5. And so the addiction began.

Intricately related to my love of all things fragrant was my obsession with my nose. For as long as I can remember, I have had an issue with it. It reminded me of my father's, and every time I thought I had come to terms with it, there would be a sneaky little reminder. When my children were small – let's face it, that's when they are the harshest and truest critics, before they develop filters (oh, who am I kidding, that never happens) – they would say, 'Mummy, you have a big nose.' So, even though more thoughtful souls would reassure me that that my nose was 'fine', I never really believed them.

I would go for months at a time without thinking of it, and then catch sight of myself at an unflattering angle, or caught like a rabbit in the headlights without my photograph face on. Remember the days before Instagram filters and angles and the delete button? Whole packets of photos opened and destroyed before anyone caught sight of them.

*THANK GOD
I HAD THAT
NOSE JOB*

My son Harrison, up until recently, had the most appalling photo of me on his camera that he refused to delete, often taunting me from his towering height of six foot four, keeping the camera just out of my reach. I can't begin to describe how bad this picture was; I didn't even look human. He thought it was hilarious to have this documented evidence; me, not so much.

However, my nose, for all intents and purposes, always performed exceptionally well on the smelling front. I come from a long line of sniffers and I've become famous for my sense of smell. Our family are renowned for sniffing everything before we buy it, read it, taste it, go out with it . . . so you can imagine my horror when, at a fragrance showing during my time as beauty director at *Madison*, I discovered that by the end, I basically couldn't smell a damn thing. The first paddle-shaped test strip, which had been dipped in Penhaligon's Blue Bell eau de toilette (all bluebells, earth and moss with a hint of cinnamon, clove and galbanum, it launched in 1978 and was a favourite of Princess Diana's), I just vaguely registered. I am always a bit of a show-off at these events as I have been to a number of fragrance workshops run by the maestro of fragrance himself, his royal highness Michael Edwards, so I am down with the way you have to bend the paddle-shaped strips to help get them closer to my nose. These blotter strips are pure and free of any contaminants, letting the fragrance speak for itself. I learnt so much from those workshops, where Michael showcased literally hundreds of both well-known and little-known scents and taught us to tease out the notes. Even with my nose functioning at full strength, after three or four fragrance dissections, nasal fatigue took over and my nose could be revived only by sniffing a bowl full of coffee beans.

*A*FTER ATTENDING A COUPLE OF THESE WORKSHOPS, Michael asked me to the inner sanctum to be part of a workshop at his home with the heavy hitters of the fragrance industry, including the head of fragrance company Givaudan, from whom I learnt that the way the brain layers meaning on to smells is called 'configural processing, a way of mapping the odour to a meaning'. This explains a lot. We were sampling the newest fragrances about to be launched on the market. This was a laborious and at the same time fascinating process, watching Michael dissect the notes to categorise the newcomers for his perfume bible, *Michael Edwards' Fragrances of the World*, which is now in its thirty-second edition. This gem is a go-to for beauty editors, perfume houses, department stores, and basically anyone who loves fragrance. Fragrances are broken down into family categories, including: aromatic, dry woods, mossy woods, woods, woody oriental, oriental, soft oriental, floral oriental, soft floral, floral, fruity, green, water and citrus. I love Michael's take on fragrance and his scent mantra: 'A great perfume is a work of art. It can lift our days, haunt our nights and create the milestones of our memories. Perfume is liquid emotion.'

*S*O, AT THE EVENT, with my finely honed nose failing me, I was starting to panic. Initially, I blamed the deadening of my number one sense on a cold. I was with my colleague Sherine Youssef and together we sampled the wares laid out enticingly before us, her whispering the categories to me as we walked the room. I nervously oohed and aahed over each strip, dredging the superlatives from my olfactory memory.

THANK GOD
I HAD THAT
NOSE JOB

I seriously thought this was a one-off and all would return to normal once my cold had abated, but disturbingly, it was not to be the case.

At first I thought I was suffering fragrance fatigue, such as happens when you can't smell the fragrance you are wearing. This happens when the senses tire after being constantly stimulated by the same scent and your nose becomes used to the smell, but that was not what was happening. I had gone from an Olympian sense of smell (a proud family tradition) to hyposmia (a reduced sense of smell), which was bad enough, to anosmia, a complete loss of smell. The decline was gradual, until I was reduced to a quivering wreck as my super-honed sense had almost completely abandoned me. Nothing could get through, noxious or pleasurable. As I gazed up at the vast array of favourite fragrances in my office I picked up YSL's Rive Gauche; I could almost retrieve the scent of this fragrance, which I had discovered at 21 at the duty-free counter while crossing the English Channel and promptly purchased, even though it meant forgoing a week's worth of meals. Rive Gauche is a delightful soft floral underpinned with orris root and sandalwood. Fortunately, even though my sense of smell was compromised, my sense of taste was still intact. This would have been the beginning of the end.

I was still in denial, but started to consult Dr Google as to what might be the cause. Nasal polyps seemed to be a common theme. These are teardrop-shaped, form in the nose or sinuses, and look uncannily like a peeled seedless grape. These little suckers are often associated with allergies and asthma. Symptoms include runny nose,

It would be a month until my sense of smell started to return – just a hint of sensation at first, and then gradually it started working again.

sneezing (tick), post-nasal drip (tick) and decreased sense of smell (double tick). Rather unfortunately, I have also developed adult-onset asthma. The shortness of breath, which I'd convinced myself was just that and nothing else, turned out to be asthma, which improved dramatically after I started taking prednisone tablets to reduce the size of the polyps in my nose to prepare them for surgery. After a barrage of allergy tests, it turned out that I am highly allergic to rye grass. The welt left on my arm by the test rivalled Uluru.

*S*o I WAS FINALLY CATAPULTED from a state of denial to a begrudging acceptance. My first port of call was an ear, nose and throat specialist, who placed an endoscope up my nose and diagnosed a veritable forest of polyps, which had seriously compromised my sense of smell. Oh, and I also had a deviated septum. I was relieved in a way, because at least there was a reason. The solution: a sinuplasty. My nasal insecurity leapt to the forefront and I blurted out that perhaps I could combine this with a nose job. The specialist said he knew just the man, who could deal with the pesky polyps and give me a 'pretty nose' into the bargain. He referred me to plastic surgeon Dr George Marcells, who could do both procedures in the one sitting.

When I went to visit him, I was in the classic position of not wanting anyone to criticise my nose except for me, so having someone else critique such an essential part of my face was pretty confronting. On the one hand, I was desperate for George to give me confirmation that the nose I had lived with for fifty years of my life was 'fine' and

*THANK GOD
I HAD THAT
NOSE JOB*

that I really didn't need anything done at all. And on the other hand, I wanted to change it. Needy old distrustful me was never far from the surface; I didn't envy George having to walk this fine line.

He navigated this delicate path with skill, however, and gave me a digitally enhanced image of what my nose would look like after the operation. George is a stickler for exactitude, thank god, and he uses techniques based on open-structure rhinoplasty. This can take longer to perform than other methods, but he believes they help keep the basic foundation of the nasal structure strong, ensuring a more predictable shape to the nose after surgery as well as improving breathing. Bingo: the old two-in-one rule that I so love.

To my delight, he turned out to be a meticulous superstar. I signed on the dotted line, figuring anyone who knew me and my penchant for putting my body on the line would figure that if I said I was having my polyps removed, they'd simply think it was code for a nose job. I nervously figured it was now or never.

I fronted up for the surgery, justifying it to myself as being two-birds-one-stone. The actual procedure was very intense, as it involved peeling back the skin of the nose to get better access to the nasal structure, ensuring a 'predictable shape' and improved breathing. It is a bit like lifting the bonnet of a car and then filing away at the structure underneath to get the right shape. I had stupidly watched a video of this procedure recently. I am not quite sure why – once I had committed to the challenge, there was no looking back. I told my husband that along with the polyp removal I was also having my deviated septum straightened (which was true!), hence the procedure would be more expensive and the recovery period longer.

I woke up in recovery after six hours of surgery with a giant supportive splint on my nose, as well as internal nasal splints and two massive tampon-like packs up each nostril. This was not a procedure for the faint-hearted. When George came to give me the nod to be discharged, he kind of blew my cover when he asked my husband what he thought of my newly shaped nose. I was spluttering 'Deviated septum!' and 'Polyps!', though, so I hope it washed over him. Once I was home, the first hurdle was getting to the seven-day mark, when the packing would come out. Bizarrely, having to breathe through my mouth was by far the most painful part of the recovery. Nights were the worst, as my mouth became completely dehydrated and felt like cracked parchment; I had to sip water every ten minutes just to stay sane. I hadn't been this sleep deprived since my sons were babies. This part of the process was the most uncomfortable – the longest seven days of my life. I was counting down the moments until my new nose was liberated and I could finally smell. This may sound weird, but I actually wanted to smell my sons' farts again.

To keep everything clean and stop the 'crusting', scabbing inside the nose (that word alone was enough to turn my stomach), I needed to douche both nostrils with a sinus solution mixed with steroid ointment eight times a day. The whole process was pretty vile, as giant clots of blood that seemed to go on forever emerged from both my nostrils. By 2 a.m. each night the demons were in full swing. I sent an emergency text to a friend overseas who talked me down, saying the packing was the worst and it would be such a joy when it came out. Sherine visited me and laughed, saying that my green and yellow panda eyes (bruising resulting from the surgery) were certainly not a beauty trend that was going to take off any time soon.

THANK GOD
I HAD THAT
NOSE JOB

There were a couple of hiccups. First, one of the stitches that had re-anchored my nose to my face came adrift, so Dr Marcells came beetling into his surgery on a Saturday to repair it. Then, in my enthusiasm to keep my nose clean, I managed to expose one of the internal grafts. I was so fastidious and freaked out about the crusting that I probably caused the problem, which then required another general anaesthetic and the reinsertion of a new graft.

The day of reckoning and the reveal finally arrived. Nurse Jackie, who had patiently talked me off many a ledge, sat me down, removed the external nose splint and then delicately removed the stitches. Next the internal splints came out, and finally the dreaded nasal stuffing. I could finally breathe through my nose again and once I looked in the mirror, I was on a super high as my remodelled septum and nose looked perfect to me. It looked like my nose, only more refined. It would be a month until my sense of smell started to return – just a hint of sensation at first, and then gradually it started working fully again.

This was only the beginning of a very long process. Basically, it took two years for my remodelled nose to finally settle in and the care required was nothing short of devotional. I had to strap my nose with tape daily, and could only take it off for special occasions, to keep the swelling at bay. It was initially challenging trying not to feel self-conscious as I walked around, but then it became a badge of honour. I remember running into the sister of one of Harrison's friends, who was with a gaggle of teenage girls. I immediately started regaling them with way too much information about what was involved in having a nose job as their faces visibly paled.

Eventually I only had to do the strapping nightly, but I had to keep it up for a whole year. The tip of my nose was where the swelling was most obvious and at each visit, George injected cortisone into the tip to try to reduce the scar tissue. Nurse Jackie warned me that George was a perfectionist and that if the swelling didn't subside, he might want to do a revision to excise the scar tissue. At each follow-up visit he would bring up the possibility. I am very susceptible to suggestion, so each time we had this conversation I would go home and question whether I should have it done.

My breathing improved brilliantly straight after the procedure and, a month in, my sense of smell started to return. Tantalisingly, it began. I was at the launch of an India Hicks fragrant body range and the first thing to break through was her Super Lily Hand Wash; the scent hit my nostrils and it was almost orgasmic. Next was a Dyptique candle in Lierre, followed by glue, Chanel No. 22, Citizen Queen, and yes, my sons' farts. The process was quite gruelling, but you know what they say, 'no pain, no gain'.

My nose did look great though, and most importantly I could smell. As I wandered through the supermarket doing the grocery shopping one morning I ran into a friend who was a nose job veteran. She gave me her best advice: no sunglasses for three months, no heavy lifting, and no extreme faces, just to keep everything in place. I mused that number three could be a stretch, as I am famous for my giveaway face. I remember being at a function that involved an intricate Power-Point presentation when a rather helpful colleague screeched across the room, 'Could you look any more bored?' Little did she realise that this was my concentrating face.

After convalescing at home for two weeks, I was overjoyed about returning to the fragrant paradise of my *Madison* office in Park

*THANK GOD
I HAD THAT
NOSE JOB*

Street. It was sensory overload for my renovated sinuses and a big outing for my new nose. With my olfactory sense restored I was ready to rediscover my ten favourite fragrances all over again.

However, three years after my operation, my sense of smell had alarmingly started to fade again. The words of a 'helpful' cab driver were ringing in my ears, as he'd overheard my conversation about my original operation and helpfully added that polyps often grow back. When I went to have it checked out, my worst fears were realised – the polyps had returned. I had a CAT scan and Nurse Jackie called me to say that George needed to sit me down and talk to me. I live on worry energy, so that was immediately heightened, but I rationalised, over and over again, trying to reassure myself, that if it was really serious, surely they would want me to go in immediately and not wait a week, right? Nevertheless, I tortured myself – and many of those around me – with worry until I was standing with George and examining the scans. There it was, the unmistakeable black space that should be clear and very obviously wasn't. The polyps had returned. It was at this moment that the decision to have had my nose job seemed even more right.

George suggested that if we were going in to scrape out the polyps then maybe he should do a revision on the tip of my nose. I could always tell at my three-monthly catch-ups that he was keen to go in again and minimise the scar tissue on the tip of my nose. Being highly susceptible to the power of suggestion I said I would think about it. Jackie talked me through what it would involve, saying the recovery would be very similar to the initial procedure with a splint worn initially and then a year of strapping my nose. I immediately canvassed every human I have ever met to gauge the response. Most said, 'Absolutely not, it is perfect as it is.' One or two suggested that as he was going in again, why not? I seesawed between yes and no but when it came down to the crunch I opted just to have the polyps removed and leave well enough alone. My sense of smell was back on track and my nose was perfect, as far as I was concerned.

This operation was shorter than the first procedure, but I still had to endure the stuffing up my nose for a week. The intense relief when that padding comes out is hard to describe. Unfortunately, nasal polyps tend to recur if the underlying irritation, allergy, or infection isn't adequately controlled, so I have to be a good patient and use the steroid douche to flush my nostrils out. I am supposed to do it twice a day and when George cross-examined me I had to admit I was doing a little less than that. He made me promise to do it at least once a day to prevent the nasal polyps from returning, and I also undergo periodic medical examinations with a nasal endoscope. I love catching up with George so this is no hardship. He always tells me about the newest plastic surgery techniques, including the revised deep plane facelift. Not quite ready for that one yet, though.

THANK GOD
I HAD THAT
NOSE JOB

SCENTSIBILITY

Olfaction is the sense of smell. Sensory cells in the nose, mouth and throat interpret smells and taste flavours, and these nerve cells are found in small patches of tissue located in a pair of clefts high inside the nose. Microscopic molecules released by food, flowers, fragrance – anything with a scent – stimulate these sensory cells and once they detect the molecules they send messages to the brain. This enables us to identify and remember an astonishing 10 000 odours. Our noses are designed to sniff out what is good for us and what is bad, so there is a reason we are attracted to jasmine tuberose, the scent of the sea or freshly cut grass, and repelled by the stench of smelly socks.

According to smell experts and Nobel Laureates Richard Axel and Linda Buck, who were awarded the prize for medicine in 2004 for their work on smell, the human nose (and our sense of smell) is capable of detecting positive qualities, for example a good wine or ripened strawberry. These positive smells activate a range of sensory odour receptors. I love this quote from Helen Keller: 'Smell is a potent wizard that transports us across thousands of miles and all the years we have lived.'

This is why olfaction is such an emotive sense. A first-smelt fragrance, a just-baked cake (this never happens in my household), freshly cut grass, wood-fire smoke, your children's hair, wet dog or garden roses all stir up potent memories. When I lost this sense I felt as if I was missing an arm, so when it was restored, my joy knew no bounds. I set about rediscovering some old favourites and introducing a few newbies to my top ten.

1. **Chanel No. 22 eau de toilette** is still my all-time favourite desert island pick. There have been some close contenders but I return to this scent time after time. I remember, vividly, smelling it for the first time on a very dear friend more than 20 years ago. It was when I was working at *Vogue* and a colleague walked past my desk; it was like a scene from *Perfume*; I was totally addicted. I staggered after her, desperate to know what her fragrance was. It reminded me of my little sons' freshly washed hair. No. 22 is a floral/oriental scent, created in 1922 by Coco Chanel; the aldehydes in the fragrance add impact and oomph to the heady notes of tuberose. This description doesn't do justice to the hypnotically addictive qualities of this gem, though. It is a sleeper in the armoury of fabulous Chanel fragrances and I kind of want to keep it that way.

2. A very close second has to be **Juliette Has a Gun's Citizen Queen Eau de Parfum.** This is a leathery chypre, created by Romano Ricci, the grandson of Nina Ricci, no less. As if I wasn't obsessed by this killer scent already, I became an even greater devotee after having dinner with the man himself. Romano was initiated into the secrets of perfumery by his grandfather, Robert Ricci. 'He had a tremendous respect for tradition and a vision of womanhood which still impresses me today. He has passed on to me the fundamentals of perfumery, but also how to transgress them,' he told me. I remember being in the supermarket (I seem to spend my life and my ill-gotten gains there, feeding my perpetually hungry sons) wearing Citizen Queen. A charming man approached me in the frozen food section – he had been trailing me since aisle one – and asked me if I could tell

*THANK GOD
I HAD THAT
NOSE JOB*

him what fragrance I was wearing, as he loved it and wanted to get it for his sister. Sherine says that whenever she smells it, it reminds her of me.

3. Having to put my babies in order is killing me, but coming in at number three would have to be **Memoire Liquide Eau de Parfum Bespoke Perfumery**, which is on file for me at Henri Bendel in New York. The first time I went in there was to get this intoxicating perfume for my editor at the time. I was so entranced by it that I secretly bought one for myself. When I returned there a couple of years later the salesgirl remembered me by name – now that is service. The creator Robin Coe-Hutshing came to Australia some time later and I had lunch with her; she introduced me to her reserve edition range. I fell in love with Amour instantly, with its enticing blend of Madagascan vanilla, tonka bean and incense. Okay, so I know that is two, but I'm counting it as one.

4. From here on in my other loves are in no particular order. They just depend on the mood of the day. **Antonia's Flowers Tiempe Passate** is pure sensuality, named after a song that Antonia's grandfather wrote. It is a musky floral with notes of amber, clementine, cedarwood, bergamot and rose. The old-fashioned stopper makes application a unique experience.

5. All of the favourites have a story behind them, which I think is what
anchors them to my heart. I was one of the last journalists to interview
fragrance goddess Annick Goutal for *Vogue* before she died, in her
beautiful house in Saint-Germain in Paris, and **Gardenia Passion**,
amongst all of her divine concoctions, was my favourite. It captures
the heady scent of blooming gardenias picked fresh from the garden
after a rain shower. Goutal was a late developer in the fragrance
stakes, having first had a career as a concert pianist. Then, in 1977,
she met nose Henri Sorsana and spent seven years honing her
talents as a new nose with him. She created each of her fragrances
as a reminder of someone or something important in her life. 'Like
precious bouquets, gathering the rarest and most noble of natural
essences, they are composed as a symphony, note by note, in an
eternal quest for balance, quality and perfect harmony,' she said.
According to Goutal, brunettes are drawn to the seductive side of
Passion (that must mean I am returning to my roots). 'A perfume
is made to give pleasure,' she said. 'Perfume is an intimate secret,
and only revealed to those who are extremely close to you.'
I remember this trip so well as my editor at the time, Marion Hume,
had asked me to bring back some highly desirable Dyptique candles
from the shop in Saint-Germain-des-Prés. On entering this Aladdin's
cave, I went into sensory overload. It was one of the most beautiful
stores I had ever been in. My order totalled six candles including
the to-die-for Figuier. I just had to up the order with one for myself.
Do you know how heavy those suckers are? I lugged them all the way
home, only to discover that Georges in Melbourne had re-opened
and was stocking, guess what, Dyptique.

THANK GOD
I HAD THAT
NOSE JOB

6. I need to have fragrance by my side at all times. My dressing table is a shrine to about 50 and I have my favourites in rollerballs so I can carry them everywhere. **Kai Eau de Parfum** is in the glove box of my car; it is the essential pick-me-up scent and always makes me think of summer, with its divine blend of gardenia and white flowers. I dab it on the pulse points on my wrists. And when I feel in the mood for a layering moment, the body cream is also to die for.

7. **Kiehl's Original Musk Eau de Toilette** is unisex and an absolute delight. This, again, has been a staple in my fragrance wardrobe: I have one beside my bed and my desk, and I travel with a mini roll-on. Addicted, somewhat. It is the perfect blend of bergamot, orange blossom, rose, lily, ylang-ylang and neroli, tonka nut, white patchouli and musk. I pulled it out on a flight back from Paris once and the woman next to me badgered me until I told her what it was. When this happens I experience the funny dichotomy of being flattered that someone can be so obsessed with the scent you are wearing, but on the flip side there is my secret self who wants to keep it strictly my signature scent.

8. Now, **Guerlain Vetiver** is an oldie but a serious goody. I have loved this fragrance ever since I did a story on women wearing men's fragrances. Vetiver is the perfectly weighted combination of fresh citrus and Haitian vetiver root, which is a woody note, and a hint of spice with pepper and nutmeg. I am in good company as Elle Macpherson is also a fan. There are so many amazing men's fragrances that are great to give the men in your life as long as you can also sneak

a spritz every now and then. Whenever I go to fragrance showings I am invariably attracted to the men's ones, grabbing my favourites for my sons to test-drive – as long as I know exactly where they are for my occasional hit.

9. **Fracas de Robert Piguet** is a huge, all-encompassing tuberose fragrance that should be worn with extreme caution as it can attract serious attention from about a hundred paces. A friend of mine had to do a deathroll from a car to escape an unwanted advance while wearing it, and I was serving drinks at a school rugby function when one of the dads leapt over the trestle table and nuzzled my neck, gasping, 'What is that?' This incredibly lush white floral has tuberose, jasmine and gardenia as top notes with a base of sandalwood and musk. It screams pheromones.

10. And finally my latest addition to the addiction list, Frederic Malle's **Portrait of a Lady**. I daren't whisper it but it has arguably become my new favourite. I smelt it on a friend a couple of years ago and it hit me right between the eyes. I kept sniffing her neck to soak up the scent. She begged me not to reveal it to anyone else and just keep it as our dirty little fragrance secret. It is an intoxicating oriental rose with a blend of benzoin, cinnamon, patchouli, musk and frankincense: the heroin of fragrance.

I am sad that I have to limit myself to just ten, as there are many, many worthy contenders.

*THANK GOD
I HAD THAT
NOSE JOB*

HOW TO WEAR

- Spray your fragrance on the palms of your hands so you get the benefit as well as those around you.
- If you are on the hunt for a new fragrance, sniff no more than three in one sitting, as your nose will go into meltdown.
- Once you have whittled it down to your new favourite, spray it into the crook of your arm and let it sit with you for a while.
- The trick is knowing that you need to like the way a fragrance smells first up, but also after it dries down.
- Don't be afraid to venture out of your comfort zone. Just because you love florals doesn't mean you can't embrace an oriental.
- Smell everything, even the unexpected scents. I remember road testing some fragrances at a sitting and one of them was based on semen. Yes, really.
- Keep your fragrances out of direct sunlight.
- Apply fragrance after you shower, but before you get dressed, so that the scent permeates your clothes.
- Educate your nose by doing a wine-tasting class. This will help you learn to pick the notes in fragrances.
- There's so much variation in individual body chemistry that no scent will smell exactly alike on two people.
- Shop for fragrance in the morning, when your sense of smell is at its best.
- In order to prevent olfactory overload, when trying to choose a fragrance, hold a wool sweater to your nose and inhale three times between each fragrance.
- Wait 15 minutes for top notes to dissipate and an hour for the fragrance to develop fully.

- Go with three to five spritzes for an eau de toilette and stay
  with the same dose even if you are tempted to up it, because your
  nose gets used to a scent and stops registering it. You don't want
  the fragrance to enter the room before you do.
- Hold the bottle as close to your skin as possible to avoid spraying
  the air rather than your skin with the fragrance.
- Wear fragrance on your pulse points (wrists, backs of knees,
  the crooks of elbows and behind your ears).
- To make the fragrance run the distance, try layering: wash with the gel,
  then apply the body lotion, and finally the fragrance itself.
- Don't rub your wrists together as it crushes the delicate scent molecules.
- And in the inimitable words of HRH Coco Chanel, just remember:
  'A woman without perfume has no future.'

THANK GOD
I HAD THAT
NOSE JOB

WE ARE FAMILY

Michael Edwards breaks down the fragrances into their four fundamental groups (floral, oriental, woody and fresh) and then their 14 fragrant sub-families in his book, *Fragrances of the World*. I was trawling through this book recently and kept sighing over the dear ones that have had a home with me and ones that I need to adopt.

FLORAL TRIBUTES

FLORALS In this group there are two entries. The first one is floral: florals can be a single note or an armful of flowers. High achievers in this category include some of my all-time favourites, such as Gardenia Passion (already raved about). If you like this one, branch out. Here are some more to try:

- **En Passant Editions de Parfums** by Frédéric Malle (lilac), 2000
- **French Lime Blossom** by Jo Malone, 1995
- **Acqua di Parma Acqua Nobile Magnolia**, 2013
- **Venetian Violet Flower Water** by Crabtree & Evelyn, 2013
- **Gardenia Les Exclusifs** by Chanel, 1925
- **Sarrasins** by Serge Lutens (jasmine), 2007
- **Frangipane** by Chantecaille, 1997
- **Aqua Allegoria Nerolia Bianca** by Guerlain (orange blossom), 2013
- **Bobbi Brown Beach**, 2002 (I wore this obsessively for six months straight)
- **Cool Water Woman Summer Seas** by Davidoff, 2014
- **Chanel No. 18 Les Exclusifs** (rose), 2007
- **Paris** by YSL, 1983 (I remember this heady number so very well. Mine was in an exquisite blingy gold bottle that came in a soft pink pouch.)
- **White Rose** by Shiseido, 1954
- **Acqua di Gioia Eau Fraiche** by Giorgio Armani (citrus fruity), 2013

- **Joy** by Jean Patou (bouquet), 1930
- **Jasmine Rouge** by Tom Ford Private Blend, 2009

SOFT FLORAL These powdery soft florals contain a heady mixture of aldehydes, flowers and notes including musk, vanilla and iris. If you like Chanel No. 5 try these bad boys:

- **Living Grace** (fresh) by Philosophy, 2012
- **Absolue Pour le Matin** by Maison Francis Kurkdjian unisex, 2010
- **Rossetto No. 14 Prada Exclusive Scents**, 2012
- **Chanel No. 5 eau Première**, 1921
- **Fieno** by Santa Maria Novella, 1886
- **Jubilation 25** by Amouage, 2007
- **Aldehyde 44** by Le Labo, 2007
- **Grand Amour** by Annick Goutal, 1997
- **Soir de Paris** by Bourjois, 1928
- **Clean Fresh Laundry** by Clean, 2004
- **Gin Fizz** by Lubin, 1955
- **Eau d'Ivoire** by Balmain, 2000
- **Liquid Cashmere** by Donna Karan, 2014
- **White Musk** by The Body Shop, 1994

ORIENTAL EXPRESS

FLORAL ORIENTAL This type blends the best of the best with orange blossom, aldehydes and spices. Remember that big beast of a fragrance, Dior Poison 1985, which left you in no doubt that whoever was wearing it was in the room? That was a floral oriental. Here are some others:

THANK GOD
I HAD THAT
NOSE JOB

- Beckham Signature Story for Women, 2009
- Jil Sander No. 4, 1990
- Gucci Guilty, 2010
- Jean Paul Gaultier, 1997
- L'Agent by L'Agent Provocateur, 2011
- L'Heure Bleue by Guerlain, 1912
- Rouge Hermès, 2000
- Burberry Brit, 2003
- Trésor by Lancôme, 1990
- Mojave Ghost by Byredo, 2014
- Rose Water and Vanilla by Jo Malone, 2010
- Mon Jasmin Noir Bvlgari, 2011

SOFT ORIENTAL Just as the name suggests, this is a softer version of its big sister with twists on incense and amber. A delicious combination in the citrus fruity category is Almond Coconut by Laura Mercier 2005. Some to experiment with:

- Naughty Alice by Vivienne Westwood, 2010
- L'Eau by Diptyque, 2013
- Ambre de Cabochard by Grès, 2007
- Coco by Chanel, 1984
- Opium by Yves Saint Laurent, 1977
- Youth Dew by Estée Lauder, 1953
- Rose Infernale by Terry de Gunzburg, 2014
- Fleur de Chocolat by Molinard, 2008
- White Patchouli by Tom Ford, 2008
- Salt Caramel by Shay & Blue, 2014

ORIENTAL Bring on the big guns: orientals are the opposite of shy, with their blend of oriental resins, rich flowers, vanilla and musk topped by green, citrus or fruity notes. Obsession by Calvin Klein is a great example of this powerful group. If you like that, try these:

- **Eau de Cristobal** by Balenciaga, 2003
- **Shalimar Parfum Initial L'Eau Si Sensuelle** by Guerlain, 2013
- **Tabu** by Dana, 1932
- **Must de Cartier** by Cartier, 1981
- **La Myrrhe** by Serge Lutens, 1995
- **Akkad** by Lubin, 2012
- **Alien Essence Absolue** by Thierry Mugler, 2012
- **Fleur Oriental** by Miller Harris, 2000
- **Oil Fiction** by Juliette Has a Gun, 2013
- **Shalimar** by Guerlain, 1925
- **Stoned** by Solange Azagury-Partridge, 2006
- **Sublime Vanille** by Creed, 2010

WOODY ORIENTAL These are sandalwood and patchouli-inflected scents. The launch of Guerlain's Samsara in 1989 will live on in beauty memory as one of the greatest and last truly global fragrance launches, held at The Oriental Hotel in Bangkok (where else). The night was steamy, lush and exotic, and filled with the sound of drums. Those were the days.

- **Coco Mademoiselle Fresh** by Chanel, 2001
- **Costume National 21**, 2008
- **Bois de Gaïac et Poire No. 4** by Miller et Bertaux, 2006

*THANK GOD
I HAD THAT
NOSE JOB*

- **Beloved Woman** by Amouage, 2012
- **Casbah** by Robert Piguet, 2012
- **Flowerbomb La Vie en Rose** by Viktor & Rolf, 2015
- **Kingdom** by Alexander McQueen, 2003
- **Le Feu d'Issey** by Issey Miyake, 1998
- **Black Cashmere** by Donna Karan, 2002
- **Hypnotic Poison** by Dior, 1998
- **Prada Amber**, 2004
- **Dune** by Dior, 1991
- **Alameda** by Robert Piguet, 2013
- **Costes** by Hôtel Costes, 2003

GETTING A HARD-ON

WOODY These are the scents that use aromatic woods, with flavours of cedar, pine, sandalwood, vetiver and patchouli. Vetiver by Guerlain is one of my all-time favourites and is equally good on men or women.

- **Gucci Oud**, 2014
- **Fig Apricot** by Fresh, 1997
- **Vetiver and Black Tea** by Kiehl's, 2014
- **Colette** by Tocca, 2010
- **Vetiver Geranium** by Creed, 2014
- **10 Corso Como** by 10 Corso Como, 1999
- **Féminité du Bois** by Serge Lutens, 1992
- **Vodka on the Rocks** by Kilian, 2014
- **India Hicks Island Living** by Crabtree & Evelyn, 2007
- **Narciso** by Narciso Rodriguez, 2014

MOSSY WOODS/CHYPRES These are fragrances with forest notes, all oakmoss and amber, patchouli and citrus. This group of wood dwellers is named after Chypre de Coty, 1917. Think sophisticated wood nymph.

- **58 Avenue Montaigne pour Femme** by S. T. Dupont, 2012
- **Darling** by Kylie Minogue, 2006
- **Halston** by Halston, 1975
- **Niki de Saint Phalle**, 1982
- **Acqua di Parma Profumo** by Acqua di Parma, 2008
- **Lady Vengeance** by Juliette Has A Gun, 2006
- **Gucci Rush** by Gucci, 1999
- **Narciso Rodriguez for Her** by Narciso Rodriguez, 2003
- **Neroli** by Roja Dove, 2012
- **Red** by Giorgio Beverly Hills, 1989
- **Mitsouko** by Guerlain, 1919

DRY WOODS Also known as chypre, the notes of these fragrances are a mixture of cedar, burnt wood and tobacco and come across all leathery. Unisex Bvlgari Black is one of my favourites, from its intoxicating smoky scent to its brilliant wheel-shaped bottle. Mine is engraved with my name. So chic – thank you, Bvlgari. Big category for the boys.

- **Aromatic Elixir** by Clinique, 1971
- **Malaise of the 1970s** by Etat Libre d'Orange, 2012
- **Patchouli 24** by La Labo, 2006
- **Eau de Hermès** by Hermès, 1951
- **Voyages en Orient: Nomaoud** by Comptoir Sud Pacifique, 2009

THANK GOD
I HAD THAT
NOSE JOB

- **Déclaration** by Cartier, 1998
- **Original Musk** by Kiehl's, 1963
- **L'Eau d'Issey Pour Homme Nuit D'Issey** by Issey Miyake, 2014
- **Aramis** by Aramis, 1965
- **Polo** by Ralph Lauren, 1978
- **Journey Man** by Amouage, 2014

FRESH AS A DAISY

AROMATIC/FOUGERE Cool and warm notes featuring lavender and citrus, spices and oriental woods blend to create these masculine fragrances: a force to be reckoned with. Strap yourself in. The aromatic Jazz by Yves Saint Laurent is a hero.

- **L'Eau Froide** by Serge Lutens, 2012
- **Safari for Men** by Ralph Lauren, 1992
- **Drakkar Noir** by Guy Laroche, 1982
- **Notes** by Robert Piguet, 2012
- **Jicky** by Guerlain, 1889
- **Royal Water** by Creed, 1997
- **Bleu de Chanel** by Chanel, 2010
- **Tommy** by Tommy Hilfiger, 1995
- **Cool Water** by Davidoff, 1988
- **Homme** by Yves Saint Laurent, 2003
- **Hugo** by Hugo Boss, 1995
- **Yacht Man Dark** by Myrurgia, 2005

CITRUS This group is all about zestiness: think lemons, mandarins, bergamot, oranges and grapefruit fresh from the branch; it is also the oldest in the fragrance family. Add to these floral, woody and spicy notes to give new depth to the light, sparkly, clean originals. Cristalle by Chanel is a keeper. So fresh, clean and crisp, it feels like an eau de cologne. Other great contenders in the citrus category include:

- **CK One** by Calvin Klein, 1994
- **Vetiver Babylone: Les Eaux** by Armani Privé, 2007
- **Green Tea** by Elizabeth Arden, 1999
- **Zeste de Vigne** by Caudalie, 2011
- **Eau de Sud** by Annick Goutal, 1977
- **Ô de Lancôme** by Lancôme, 1969
- **Calypso** by Lili Bermuda, 2013
- **4711 Original** by 4711, 1792
- **Central Park** by Bond No. 9, 2004
- **Douro Eau de Portugal (Lords)** by Penhaligon's, 1911
- **Burberry Baby Touch** by Burberry, 2002

WATER Marine, ozonic and aquatic notes define this group, which came into being in 1990 and induce visions of freshly washed clothes, sea spray and the frisson in the air before and after a thunderstorm. Pivotal fragrance in this family is the crisp L'Eau d'Issey by Issey Miyake (1992).

- **Marc Jacobs Splash: Rain** by Marc Jacobs, 2012
- **Millésime Impérial** by Creed, 1995
- **Kenzo Homme** by Kenzo, 1991

*THANK GOD
I HAD THAT
NOSE JOB*

- **Acqua di Gio Pour Homme** by Giorgio Armani, 1996
- **Escape** by Calvin Klein, 1991
- **Balenciaga Paris l'Edition Mer** by Balenciaga, 2015
- **Cambridge** by Floris by Request, 2013
- **Blue Seduction for Men** by Antonio Banderas, 2007
- **Molecule 02** by Escentric Molecules, 2008
- **L'Eau Pure** by Caron, 2014

GREEN This family draws on olfactory memories of green notes such as freshly cut grass, with an added sharpness brought to it by the distinctive resin-based galbanum. More recently the greenness has been softened with the addition of softer notes to make the family more accessible. I was introduced to Eau de Campagne by Sisley (1974), by a colleague famous for pushing the boundaries and this fragrance is no exception, with its distinctive tomato-leaf base.

- **Play Green** by Comme des Garçons, 2012
- **L'eau du Trente-Quatre** by Diptyque, 2013
- **Eau de Sisley 2** by Sisley, 2009
- **Aliage** by Estée Lauder, 1972
- **Vent Vert** by Balmain, 1947
- **Untitled L'Eau Maison Martin Margiela**, 2011
- **One Love** by Jean-Louis Scherrer, 2015
- **Gramercy Park** by Bond No. 9, 2003
- **Live** by Lacoste, 2014

FRUITY This group is a fruit salad of berries, peaches, pears, plums and apples, mixed with an abundance of floral notes. Ralph by Ralph Lauren (2000) is the innovator on the fruity fragrance frontier. It's a tight category with a boutique number of entries.

- **Creed Pour Enfants** by Creed, 2016
- **360° Coral for Women** by Perry Ellis, 2014
- **Blackberry & Bay** by Jo Malone, 2012
- **Angel Eau Sucrée** by Thierry Mugler, 2015
- **Hippie Princess** by Vera Wang, 2015
- **Pulp** by Byredo, 2007
- **Eau Spontanée** by L'Occitane, 2013
- **1804 George Sand** by Histoires de Parfums, 2000
- **Mora Bella (Fruit Savages)** by Comptoir Sud Pacifique, 1987
- **Hearts and Daggers For Women** by Ed Hardy, 2009

*THANK GOD
I HAD THAT
NOSE JOB*

CELEBRITIES: UP CLOSE AND PERSONAL

THE JOYS OF MY JOB, which are legion, have also included interviews with some spectacular people. I have loved them all, but one stands out as deeply memorable. It was with the one and only Jane Fonda in the one and only Ritz Hotel, Place Vendôme in Paris. I was there on assignment with *Madison* for L'Oréal Paris (I know, I know), with beauty editor Dani Jackson from *Who Weekly*. There were big celebrations for the 40-year anniversary of the L'Oréal Paris slogan, 'Because I'm Worth It' and the paean to self-esteem is still going strong, having morphed into 'Because You're Worth It'. We are staying at our 'usual', the Sofitel Paris Le Faubourg, 15 rue Boissy d'Anglas. I love this hotel; it is so close to shopping central on the corner of the rue du Faubourg Saint-Honoré and in the break between interviewing superstars, there was much credit card damage committed.

So, to set the scene, we had three interviews that day with the L'Oréal Paris ambassadors: one with actor Freida Pinto, one with Jane Fonda and the other with famous amputee athlete and all-round phenomenal person, Aimee Mullens (check out her TED Talks) to talk about everything from beauty to kookaburras.

As we milled around outside the Ritz in that beautiful square waiting to go in, an amazing suit walked up behind us and in it (I think it was a YSL, actually) was none other than Kate Moss, who was with her husband Jamie Hince. I actually think she might have been checking out my Saint Laurent Tributes, to be honest. We all tried not to stare, without much success, as they waited for a cab. This set the high-octane tone for what was to come.

I always get nervous before interviews, even after all these years. The PR said how surprising this was as I had done so many, but each interview is still a really big thing for me. It is a mark of respect to the interviewee and I'm always a bit starstruck, each and every time. All the journalists from around the world gather in an anteroom awaiting their slot, so there's lots of time for excitement to mount. This occasion was no exception. First cab off the rank was Freida Pinto, best known for her portrayal of Latika in *Slumdog Millionaire*. I had also watched her in *Planet of the Apes* on the flight over. Dani and I were grouped together in the one interview, which was great as Dani is warm and endearing and always asks great questions. Doing an interview with another journalist is a very different dynamic, as you have to make sure you get your fair share of questions and time in; this is where Kate, our wrangler, kept everything fair. Dani and I were a good tag team on this trip in all senses – we shopped, we ate, we drank (Sancerre).

We were ushered into a plush, pistachio-coloured suite where Freida was waiting and I am here to tell you that while she is gorgeous on-screen, she is even more beautiful off, dressed in a Reed Krakoff chamois-coloured sequinned dress with red piping. She was totally captivating as she talked about her favourite red carpet moments, one of which was the BAFTAs in 2009, when she was nominated for *Slumdog*. She wore a pink Oscar de la Renta dress that he custom made for her so it fit like a glove. She referred to it nostalgically as her 'princess moment'.

To top it off she wore an 18th-century Fred Leighton jewellery piece, and she laughed that she had to be very careful with it.

Slumdog was a defining moment for her as an actor and she shared the insight that being a part of the film industry has made her 'smarten up'. I remember her reflecting that it made her do things much faster than normal. My last question was one of those formulaic ones that sound a bit trite but always evinces an interesting response. I asked her, 'What is the most valuable lesson you have learned?' She replied, 'I have made loads of mistakes and at the end of every mistake there has been a great learning experience. I guess the one thing that I have learned from all of that is to just keep it real.'

We had an hour to wait before we interviewed Jane Fonda, so of course it had to be lunch in the gilded hotel restaurant, which just oozed opulence. Now here's the thing: if I am not fed and watered regularly when I am travelling things can go a bit pear-shaped; fortunately my colleagues embrace this. I was pumped from talking to Freida and couldn't wait to meet Jane. Dani and I were like kids, full of expectation and, of course, I was nervous as hell all over again.

Jane – where to begin? At 74 she is one hot mama. She was resplendent in a micro-mini with a pair of thigh-high tooled boots that she told us were 20 years old, teamed with a red-and-black sequinned jacket. She looked totally amazing and I was in total awe. We talked about her love of Australia and snorkelling on the Great Barrier Reef off Hayman Island, visiting the Daintree and her favourite bird, the kookaburra. She made me feel totally at ease. She even held my hand at one point and I have published photographic evidence to prove it. Jane was also very upfront about what works for her, beauty-wise. She

works out every day and was open about having had plastic surgery on the bags under her eyes and a little bit under the chin. She has been married three times, first to French director Roger Vadim, then to politician Tom Hayden followed by CNN founder Ted Turner, and now has a boyfriend, record producer Richard Perry. She said that being in love with Richard keeps her looking beautiful. 'At seventy-four, I have never had such a fulfilling sex life.'

On the ageing front she also said, 'I didn't want them to get rid of my wrinkles. When a woman feels good about herself and is powered from inside it shows. You can be perfect physically and have lots of plastic surgery, but if you're not happy and you don't feel good about yourself, it's going to show in your eyes. So I put a lot of credit down to attitude.

'I've also found out that after fifty, most people – rich, poor, men, women, married, not married – tend to be happier when they get a little older, which is not what we're brought up to think.' Jane has a lived a very full life and is happy to share her tips, such as combating jet lag by going for a walk or doing a yoga class, and when on board a flight, not to drink too much alcohol or eat very much – although she jokes that 'coming from Australia, the flight is so long you'd starve to death.' She is very vocal about her love of Australia and wants to see more of it. The outback is definitely on her bucket list.

For her, relaxation is key to a happy life and climbing mountains is top of the list, 'I'm happiest at about fourteen thousand feet. I like being up where the air is very thin. I've done that quite often in life and I look forward to trying to do it again. I don't know if I can. You know, I have a fake hip, a fake knee. I'm becoming a bionic woman; the airports hate me.' Jane lives very much in the present and her favourite decade, not surprisingly, is the one she is in right now. She talked about Picasso, who said that it takes a long time to become young. 'And I think that is true; I feel younger in my spirit than I did when I was young, and way happier, and it's totally not what I expected.'

I'm sure I sound like a sycophant but I gleaned lots of life lessons from our brief half-hour with her. This was a pearler: 'It's more important to be interested than interesting. People spend a lot of time wanting to be interesting, but to be interested in life and everything and who you are and how come those flowers ended up the colour that they are . . . I think staying interested keeps you young.'

We went on to talk about favourite colours and she told me that she likes to wear colour. 'When you get older it's good to wear brights,' she said. And one of the highlights of our interview was when we talked about guilty pleasures; top of Jane's list was, 'A really good cheeseburger. You know, my favourite ex-husband, Ted Turner, and I would travel a lot. He had a plane and we always knew where the best hamburgers were all over the United States. And they were in weird places, in little towns in Nebraska.'

W E WERE RUNNING OUT OF TIME and there was so much I still wanted to ask her. She told me that Robert Redford, whom she calls 'Bob', was her favourite male actor to work with. She did three movies with him: *The Chase*, *Barefoot in the Park* and *The Electric Horseman* and loved every minute. We finished the interview with a question

I always ask: 'What is your life mantra?' '"This too shall pass." This is a concept that is very hard for young people. It's so hard to be young because you think, "Oh my god this crisis is going to kill me," but when you get older it's like, "Oh, I've been there: this too shall pass." Almost nothing stresses me any more. If I feel stress coming, I just breathe and let it pass. Stress is what kills you. It's really important to know how to get rid of all of the stress.' Note to self: try to take this mantra on board.

The day had so much packed into it (see, I do actually do some work) and we still had one interview left, with the remarkable Aimee Mullens. What to expect? She walked into the room, a long cool vision wearing the most astonishing pair of Miu Miu heels. She began by telling us that she has dozens of sets of prosthetic legs, all in different lengths. 'Yeah, I can be as tall as I want to be with all these legs,' she laughed. Her candour is so disarming and endearing, she is inspiring company.

Track record: Aimee Mullins is an athlete, activist and model who had her legs amputated as a result of fibular hemimelia (no fibular bone) at the age of one. She is a stellar person, with more determination than anyone I have ever met. Her accolades include Olympic athlete, fashion model and muse, actress, lobbyist and charity worker. Her drive to succeed began early. After finishing school with honours, Aimee was one of only three students in the US chosen for a full academic scholarship from the Department of Defence and, at 17, she became the youngest person to hold a top-secret security clearance at the Pentagon, where she worked as an intelligence analyst, deep underground, during her summer holidays.

At Georgetown University, Aimee embarked upon an athletic career. She competed in the 1996 Paralympics in Atlanta with prosthetic legs modelled after the hind legs of a cheetah, and went on to set world records in the 100 metres, 200 metres and long-jump events. And in 2007, Aimee became the president of the Women's Sports Foundation. She has also modelled for Alexander McQueen and, in 1999, she became his muse and walked the runway in his London show sporting intricately carved wooden prosthetic boots. There is an infamous story that Aimee tells of Naomi Campbell demanding to wear the boots, as she was the head model. Aimee replied that the boots had been custom-made for her. Aimee was also named one of the 50 Most Beautiful People by *People* magazine. We could have sat and listened all day.

*P*ARIS REALLY IS THE HEARTLAND OF BEAUTY FOR ME. I have had so many astonishing trips there and met incredibly beautiful and talented people. They really always are pinch-me-moments and I love revisiting them as I write this book. Another career highlight came when I was working for *Madison* and I interviewed Anne Hathaway for Lancôme in Paris, for the launch of their fragrance Magnifique in 2008. This time I was the only journalist from Australia. Everyone knows I love a minder and mine, Christine, was the minder par excellence as we skidded around Paris in a car with our fabulous chauffeur Alex, getting our bearings – oh and doing some shopping.

The fragrance launch was held in the heart of Paris, at the then newly refurbished Galeries Nationales du Grand Palais on the Avenue

CELEBRITIES:
UP CLOSE
AND PERSONAL

des Champs-Élysées, an intricate web of towering pistachio-green vaulted steel and the largest glass roof in Europe. This stratospheric black-tie launch was the first function to be held since its renovation. Alex dropped us just outside and we were met by serious wall-to-wall glamour. After taking in the spectacular space, champagne in hand, we were ushered into the 'gala' dinner to meet the new face of Magnifique, actress Anne Hathaway. The room was swathed in luxe ruby red, with candles everywhere. After everyone was seated the ground opened up and Anne Hathaway emerged, like a phoenix, from an underground vault. Sixty black-clad waiters then glided down the grand staircase carrying bottles of the intoxicating new fragrance, Magnifique, for us to inhale.

Master perfume makers, Olivier Cresp and Jacques Cavallier, took three and a half years to create the seductive sparkling blend of florals, woods and spices that make up Magnifique. The idea was to borrow from traditionally masculine woody notes and create a 'spicy harmony for women'. Cavallier and Cresp were in India and 'just by chance' discovered an unknown woody note, nagarmotha (derived from papyrus), only a few weeks before the briefing from Lancôme. Nagarmotha is 'smooth and smoky with hints of leather', and this was combined with Australian sandalwood, vetiver, Bulgarian and Mai de Grasse rose, jasmine and saffron. In each bottle of Magnifique is the essence extracted from more than a thousand roses.

The next day, enveloped in a cloud of the heady Magnifique, Christine and I headed to the Hôtel Ritz to interview Anne Hathaway. As usual the flurry of nerves had surfaced again, but as soon as I was ushered into Hathaway's shabby-chic suite to meet her, she charmed me immediately. I had done my research and discovered that she had a chocolate labrador called Esmeralda, so I showed her a picture of my two chocolate labs, Mars and Milo – well, they are my sons' dogs, actually, but I wasn't going to let that stand in the way of relationship building. There was cooing all round as we sang the praises of this amazing breed. 'They are the best dogs in the whole wide world,' we agreed. Anne was so relaxed that she kicked off her shoes and so it began. She is very well spoken and endearingly self-deprecating, with the most gorgeous smile. Her film portfolio is also very impressive and varied: *Princess Diaries, Brokeback Mountain, Becoming Jane, Love and Other Drugs, One Day, Rachel Getting Married, The Devil Wears Prada, Get Smart, Bride Wars, Interstellar, The Dark Knight Rises, Les Misérables* . . . the list goes on.

The first thing we talked about was shoes. 'I do love a heel, especially when I am going out. But after last night I am confined to the ground,' she said. We talk about her first fragrance, which was Love's Baby Soft by Dana, aimed at teenagers, with notes of vanilla, musk, lavender and lilac. 'It never smelt good on me,' she reflected. 'Then I used The Body Shop's Beach Body Spray for a while. Back then I thought the more perfume you put on the more attractive you were to boys, so I just went around smelling like some chemical experiment. After that I searched for years to find a perfume and this one [Magnifique], I have to say, really suits me and I know that sounds like such a line, but it's true.'

We talk about favourite flowers: ranunculus, peonies and roses; and smells that evoke emotion for her. Anne says that cut grass reminds her of her youth, as she grew up in the suburbs. 'I always love

the smell in the spring right after it rains: that kind of new-earth aroma. My grandmother's house also had a real odour. It was kind of musty but it was really delicious too.' I was compelled to ask her about *The Devil Wears Prada*, as it was such a defining moment. 'I haven't really spent any time in Europe since it came out, and to see normally austere women running to get a photo because they work in fashion or PR or advertising and they wanted a picture with the girl from *The Devil Wears Prada*, it was so sweet,' she says.

'I still get nervous around designers because they have a coolness factor that I am sorely lacking. More so than becoming fashion obsessed, I become obsessed with people like Patricia Field, Agnès B — people who have that out-there, innate sense of style. Isn't Patricia fabulous! She is one of my favourite people on the planet. We need more people like her, like Vivienne Westwood. People that push boundaries and do whatever the hell they want.'

We talked about some of her favourite films and she reveals that *Becoming Jane* was one of the toughest roles she's ever had. 'I wish I could go back and remake that film. I thought that if I gave myself more than a month to perfect the accent, that would be fine, but if I could go back again I would have started three months beforehand. I was always self-conscious about it.' Her honesty and openness are infectious. As the interview wound up, Christine, who had been snapping away, captured Anne at her relaxed best, barefoot on the sofa.

On our way out we ran into Anne's brother Michael, who showed me a picture of Esmy (Anne's labrador) and Go Go (her brother's French bulldog) tucked up asleep in bed. Hilarious. So we came full circle; it was all about the dogs.

Fast forward to October 2008 and I am winging my way to New York for an audience with Dame Edna Everage to talk about her new cosmetics range, which she has developed with M.A.C. The flight getting there and the sheer, unbridled joy of flying business class and watching back-to-back movies makes turning right all the harder when we travel as a family. So spoilt, I know. There is some merit in being one of the oldest members of the beauty fraternity. Back in the 80s you didn't go on a business trip unless it was business class. Well, hey, isn't that why it was invented? Especially, if you are flying for 26 hours and will only be spending two nights at your destination.

Landing at JFK is always an event filled with expectation. The energy, the shopping (recurring theme), the interview . . . I arrived in the evening and checked in at 60 Thompson Street Hotel, Soho, slap-bang in the middle of mega shopping: the signature Prada store, Burberry, Chanel, Dolce & Gabbana, Marni, Marc Jacobs . . . My room was cool, decked out with white gladioli, a tribute to the Dame. Jo Di Loreto (you guessed it, New York-based M.A.C PR and Darling minder) and I arrived at the Milk Studio in the Meatpacking District and proceeded to get ourselves slightly lost in the labyrinth of corridors. All of a sudden, none other than Patricia Field, that beacon of stylists and the force behind the styling for *Sex and the City* and *The Devil Wears Prada* popped up and helpfully pointed us in the right direction. She was there styling the Dame for her out-there M.A.C advertising campaign. As we rounded the corner, we were engulfed in a seething bevy of minders and M.A.C people and behold, there was the Dame being wheeled in a barrow through a field of gladioli by a bare-chested man wearing a rabbit's head for the advertising campaign for the new Dame Edna

range. Miles Aldridge was the photographer, Honey did the Dame's nails, and hair and makeup was done by Wendy Fyfe. Nothing but the best for the Dame.

My nervousness level was elevated to new heights. Before leaving Sydney I had spoken to my uncle, who went to university with Barry Humphries and acted with him in the notorious 1974 film *Barry McKenzie Holds His Own*, where Barry Humphries played multiple roles, including Edna. I asked him to put in a good word for me and I also let Barry's people know that I was Mike Newman's niece. I hoped this might work in my favour. Note to self: remember to always refer to Dame Edna as herself, NOT Barry Humphries, whom she refers to as her 'entrepreneur'.

Even though I had prepared questions, which had been vetted and screened, the Dame launched into her monologue and I could barely get a word in edgeways. We were perched on director's chairs in her dressing room during a break between filming for the cosmetics campaign, and I have to confess she was incredibly compelling in her azure-blue, diamante-encrusted frock and bejewelled beige pumps, and not for a moment did I think of her as anyone but Dame Edna. I learned that she likes designers Alexander McQueen and Galliano. Very fashion forward. Behind me was a row of around 15 people monitoring the interview, including James Gager, senior vice-president and creative director of M.A.C. He raved about the new Dame Edna range, saying, 'The lilac packaging is very Dame Edna and whenever we do a collection with a star we sit with that person and really get a lot of inspiration from them. Dame Edna is very fond of lilac, signature glasses and little sparks of glitter. The makeup colours themselves are very wearable. The packaging might seem outrageous but the colours are very wearable and on trend.' I finally managed to get my first question out. When did she become a dame?

'I became a dame in the seventies, a long time ago when Mr Whitlam was prime minister of Australia during his very brief reign in which he managed to almost bankrupt Australia. He made me a dame and that was pretty well the end of his career. But the Queen recognised it. I stay with the queen in London at Buckingham Palace, and the Queen's centrally located. I've got my own shelf in the fridge there and I left a little bag of M.A.C cosmetics for her so she might be looking a bit more radiant next time you see her.' Dame Edna is irrepressible and totally captivating. M.A.C is renowned for its left-of-centre model choices and she certainly pushes this boundary. When talking about M.A.C signing her, she says:

'It would be foolish of me to think that I am a young woman, I am a mature woman and to think that of all the women in the world I have been chosen as an ambassadress for the M.A.C range, for the most cutting-edge cosmetic range in the world – I wonder what criteria they used. I had to give some examples of my skin because skin is the largest organ in the body. Would you like to touch my largest organ?' So naughty, right from the get-go. My mouth was opening and closing like a fish and then out of nowhere, 'How's Harrison? Is he still at Cranbrook?'

I was gobsmacked. Harrison, my oldest son, was then a student at Sydney's Cranbrook School and I wondered how she got this information. Later I learned that Dame Edna is famous for her incredibly well-oiled research machine and that she has gleaned information about

me from various colleagues at home in Sydney. I spluttered something in reply and turned around to look quizzically at the PR, Jo. Before I had time to regain my composure Dame Edna shot this at me:

'You're wearing your high heels again. Wasn't it funny, that incident that happened when that pigeon tried to mate with your shoe?' What? This happened at a Christmas drinks down on the quay near the Opera House. I remember distinctly what I was wearing that night: a red Karen Walker skater dress and Helmut Lang black suede stilettos with a horsehair tail. They were deeply fabulous. A pigeon took a shine to them and started to hump the tail, and I just couldn't shake him off. It was hilarious. What the hell, how did the Dame know this? *I'm seriously going to kill those girls when I get home*, I thought. 'Do you remember that? I am very well researched, aren't I? No, don't be frightened. I think I should pay people a compliment by finding out all about them,' she said.

I finish with my life mantra question. 'I wear life like a very loose garment. I never feel pressured. I do yoga. I do Pilates. And I do my pelvic floor exercises!'

I reeled out of the interview, only to run into the Dame's wife, Lizzie Spender. I was still so under the influence of her character that when she asked me if Barry was nearly done, I paused, thinking 'Who's Barry?'

After the interview Jo and I beetled down to beauty hot spot The M.A.C Pro Store, in the Flatiron District. This is beauty mecca and a honey pot for professional makeup artists from around the world, and us.

INCE I'VE BEEN IN MY LATEST INCARNATION as beauty director for *Sunday Life*, the colour supplement in the *Sun Herald* and *The Sunday Age*, I've had even more celebrity one-on-ones. Again, my M.A.C friends organised an interview for me, this time with the singing sensation and Grammy award-winner Lorde, who was 17 at the time, in her native Auckland, New Zealand. Born Ella Marija Yelich-O'Connor, she is equally famous for her knockout bold lips as for her singing and songwriting, and she was collaborating with M.A.C to launch her very own signature lipstick, named for her album *Pure Heroine*. Her achievements, even at this young age, were impressive to say the least. At five she discovered singing and acting; at 13 she signed with Universal Music Group; she is the first New Zealand artist ever to top the US hot 100; and she is on the *Forbes* list of '30 under 30 who are changing the world'.

As part of my interview prep for Lorde, I canvassed my questions with my highly musically evolved son Harrison, who was 21 at the time. I jokingly suggested that I ask her why wasn't she in school and he threatened to lynch me if I dared do such a thing. He ordered me not ask too many beauty questions as, I quote, 'She is against retouching.' Both my sons were pretty impressed that I was interviewing her. In preparation, I listened to *Pure Heroine* in the car. Lorde's voice is astonishingly moving and the lyrics are wise beyond her years. I have to agree with Elton John, who said the song 'Tennis Court' was 'one of the most beautiful things on earth'.

I was and am in awe of her poise and charm. She was wearing a fabulous cerise Valentino suit with her tousled mane of long dark hair, and the standout lips she is famous for were coated in her new M.A.C lipstick Pure Heroine. The colour was intense, a deep almost-black

CELEBRITIES:
UP CLOSE
AND PERSONAL

purple that worked perfectly against her porcelain skin. I could have passed for a M.A.C soldier myself that day, as I was in a top-to-toe black Ellery suit paired with my brand-new platform Gucci boots, which Lorde took a liking to. She spoke of the birth of the lipstick, saying, 'I picked the colour as well as the finish, as that was important to me. I obviously have a makeup artist to put my lipstick on for me, but I wanted it to be versatile for teenage girls to use and to be able to pat a little bit on like a stain, or go for full lipstick, or change the colour slightly with different liners.'

This new lipstick is a follow-up to the original Heroine, which some of the M.A.C girls were wearing and is more lavender in colour. In typical fashion I wanted to add that shade to my gigantic lipstick collection as well. Writing about it now makes me want to wear it. That is how it rolls with me, I am highly suggestible, but that is what makes the beauty universe so enjoyable. There are so many new concoctions that sometimes it is hard to know where to begin and end. On that trip I came back with three new favourite lipsticks: Heroine, Pure Heroine and a colour called Fabby, which was in a makeup kit that had been kindly placed in my room. Fabby is a ridiculously good colour: a pinky nude with a shimmer. When I got home I misplaced it and couldn't remember its name. I searched high and low, tortured the M.A.C girls to see if they could find out the shade, and even went into a M.A.C store to

I always get nervous before interviews, even after all these years. Each interview is still a really big thing for me. It is a mark of respect to the interviewee and I'm always a bit starstruck, each and every time.

try and describe it. I came out with two lipsticks but they weren't the right one. Obsessive? Slightly. Fortunately, Fabby turned up in my car so my addled mind was put to rest.

Lorde's secret makeup weapon is her makeup artist Amber D, who first met Lorde in 2013 when they worked together on her live show. The pair got on so famously that the next step was Amber doing her makeup for her album *Pure Heroine*, and the rest is history. Amber has been with Lorde ever since, creating versions of her signature bold lip for her shows, the Grammys, the *Late Show with David Letterman*, the Brit Awards and so on.

When I told Lorde that my sons were very impressed that I was going to interview Lorde in her hometown, she laughed and said, 'Tell them I was really scary and frowned all the time.' Let me tell you, the exact opposite was true.

Next came some lessons from Amber D on how to master Lorde's wicked lipstick look as well as a few other tips and tricks. 'When I perform,' said Lorde, 'I need my lipstick to be rock solid so I've got very good at drinking out of my water bottle in a certain way.' Amber regaled me with tales of sitting perched on the arm of a plane seat, getting Lorde photo-ready for touchdown.

The next day we headed into Auckland to Meadowlark Jewellery. Lorde is a big fan and often wears their designs. They had made me a beautiful individualised pair of sterling silver earrings to mark my time in New Zealand. Before we headed back to Sydney we were helicoptered over to Waiheke Island for a delicious vineyard lunch. Flying over the golden sands of Oneroa and Little Oneroa beach was a visual feast.

CELEBRITIES:
UP CLOSE
AND PERSONAL

*O*NE OF MY LAST PARIS ENCOUNTERS, to date, was with actor Naomi Watts, who was 46 at the time, for her unveiling as L'Oréal Paris's latest ambassador. I was there for one of the few one-on-one interviews with her. The Ritz was being renovated so our venue was the newly renovated Peninsular Hotel in Avenue Kléber, which was a vision, all light and golden.

Again there was lots of milling about, so there was time to stress a little. Next thing I knew, I was sofa-side with the petite, Chloé-clad Naomi. My opening gambit was about the shoes she'd been wearing at the launch the night before, which I had pegged as YSL. I'd immediately made a beeline for Galeries Lafayette to purchase a pair. They are a super-fine vanilla patent sandal. It turned out, though, when I asked Naomi about what she was wearing, the suit was Saint Laurent but the shoes were, in fact, Calvin Klein. I am more than happy with my Classic Jane Ankle Strap Sandal, though. I can never have too many Saint Laurent shoes. I asked Naomi who her favourite designers were. Isabel Marant for every day – 'I love her textures', and also Stella McCartney and Chloé.

Next we talked films. My personal favourite of Naomi's is *The Impossible*, based on the heart-wrenching story of a Spanish family who were holidaying in Thailand and managed to survive the 2004 tsunami that wreaked devastation. I have seen it numerous times, the first as a preview in a tiny screening room with six other journalists. We all came out speechless.

Naomi talked about memorable films for her. '*King Kong* was the most obvious glamour moment of any movie I have done; there were so many great beauty close-ups. The 30s era for women was remarkable for makeup and hair.' She then went on to say that while filming, she fell backwards into a crevice littered with pipes. 'It was a very scary fall; it could have been curtains, as I banged my head on pipes at the bottom. I remember coming to with my dress over my head and looking up and seeing everyone looking at my underwear. I think my yoga fitness probably saved me.'

She splits her time between Sydney, London and New York and feels equally at home in each city. Naomi tries to make time to relax by getting massages when she can. She says, 'On the weekend I go to the park or the beach with the kids. I've got a house at the beach and it's nice to get away from New York, which is fun but an exhausting city.'

As a newly minted L'Oréal Paris ambassador, when I ask her about her life mantra she laughs and says, '"Because I'm worth it." Give yourself a pat on the back and embrace the best things about yourself. Feels like a good mantra to have at the back of your mind.'

BEAUTY LOWDOWN

I have gleaned some essential beauty tips from each of the fabulous people I have interviewed, including, in some cases, what not to do. Read on.

Best makeup artist beauty tip

'The one thing I learnt from Charlotte [Tilbury] is not to pull the eyeliner out too much, even though it is a big trend in India.'

Best piece of beauty advice your mother or grandmother passed on

'The one thing the two of them never applied was sunblock.'

So this is an anti-tip?

'Yes, they told me to never do that, so I *always* apply sunblock!'

Best hair tip

'I tend to do protein treatments as often as I can because my hair is constantly being styled. Ever since I was a teenager I have used Absolute Repair by L'Oréal Professional. It's just amazing.'

Relaxation techniques

'I get reflexology treatments. I also try to eat healthily and just drink loads of water and keep hydrated. Sleep is also essential.'

Go-to beauty products

'I use L'Oréal Paris Age Re-perfect. When you get older, your skin gets drier; the products are just amazing for older skin.'

Best beauty tips

'It's funny, because I was just saying to the girl who did my makeup this morning how lucky we are, we wake up and we have these pros putting on our makeup and we can learn so much. See how I'm all dark around my eyes with kohl? Well, I never would have done that, I wouldn't have known how to do that, but I learned it from somebody about a month ago and I like it.'

Lipstick like

'Colour Riche from the Star Secrets collection.'

Beauty mantra

'Avoid stress and sleep a lot. I sleep eight or nine hours a night.
For me, sleep is really important.'

Beauty routine

'I pay more attention. When I was younger in the sixties and seventies and I was an activist, I never took time to even look in the mirror. You know, I'd comb my hair, I'd never even do the back of my head. I never did any glamour shoots. I didn't even have a facial till I was about forty-eight years old, when someone said to me, "You know, I think you should pay attention." It's weird because now that I'm older, I'm doing fashion shoots, I'm looking at the back of my head, I pay attention to my skin and you know, this is all new to me. I am sort of glad that I never spent a lot of time worrying about it when I was young. When I look at pictures of myself at the age when most people are in their beauty prime, I wasn't so good. [Are you joking?] I look better now than I did back then. [She looks fantastic now and then!] So, I don't know, now, I pay more attention.'

*CELEBRITES:
UP CLOSE
AND PERSONAL*

ANNE HATHAWAY

Desert island beauty products

'Well, of course, anything SPF60+. When you can rival Nicole Kidman in the paleness department, you know that you need a very strong sunscreen and I would bring self-tanner just in case I got rescued. And probably Rosebud Salve. You can use it as moisturiser, you can use it on burns. I have a dermatologist in New York, Dr Patricia Wexler, and so I pretty much use all of her stuff.'

Relaxation tips

'If I don't have time to really let go, I would rather do little quick fixes than try to schedule in a full detoxifying massage that I am not going to be able to really enjoy. A huge thing for me is just sitting and listening to music. Sometimes I can be a monk and just not call anyone and then I realise I need balance in my life. I just need to get out of my own head. So when I really have time to relax I like massages and going to the ocean.'

DAME EDNA

Beauty pedigree

'I'm not a conventional beauty, but I am an attractive woman. Beauty fades, attractiveness enriches itself like a fine old vintage, and there's no question about it, people are drawn to me. Since the death of my husband, I have had approaches of all kinds from very very interesting people and that was before I was wearing M.A.C. By the way, I wore M.A.C early on in my shows, little knowing that I would be chosen as their international representative.'

Lipstick or lip gloss?

'I'm a lip gloss girl. I use the minimum – so lucky.'

Favourites in your makeup range

'There is a beautiful brown which is called Wombat, Kangarouge is another, and Possum Nose Pink Lip Gloss.'

Beauty secrets

'I don't have really many beauty secrets, because I think beauty is something within and cosmetics just enhance it. I wake up in the morning and I do my G spots. Do you know what they are? I look in the mirror and I say: "You're gorgeous, you're gorgeous, you're gorgeous." '

Makeup tips

'I apply my own makeup. I think you find successful people don't have an entourage. It's only amateurs that surround themselves with armies of people, so I put my own makeup on, which means I get the lovely M.A.C product into my fingers and onto my skin. I wear a little night cream and I sometimes I use old-fashioned things, like lemon juice, for the armadillo elbows.'

LORDE

Favourite fragrance

'Acqua di Parma Colonia.'

Glowy skin

To get Lorde's skin looking glowy and dewy, her makeup artist Amber starts with a touch of concealer on any trouble spots. The next step is M.A.C Prep + Prime Highlighter in Radiant Rose on the high spots like cheekbones, followed by a light dusting of powder on the T-zone. A dab of So Sweet Easy Cream Blush on cheeks adds a brightening touch of colour.

CELEBRITES:
UP CLOSE
AND PERSONAL

Eye makeup

Amber says the neutral taupe shade, Groundwork Paint Pot, is universally
flattering and goes on creamy but won't crease. This is great worn on its own or
as a base for building extra colour. The second string of Lorde's range is Rapid
Black Penultimate Eye Liner, used to hug the lash line. Lorde's lashes
are quite straight so Amber curls them before applying mascara.

Lip service

The first step is to fill in the entire lip with a wine-coloured lip pencil, then
resharpen the pencil to create a defined perimeter. Finally, the intensely bold
lipstick is applied using a concealer brush to make sure the colour looks precise
and remains in place. To keep Lorde's lipstick in place while she performs,
Amber applies the lipstick, then places a single ply of tissue onto the lips
and pushes face powder through to create a matte lipstick effect.

Eyeliner tips

'You can't go wrong with a felt tip. They're the best for beginners.
I hold my eye up to get access to the lid,' says Lorde.

No-fuss hair

'I don't really style it. I scrunch in a bit of product when it's wet
and let it do its thing.'

Nailing it

'I do a nude a lot of the time as it goes with everything, but I use
dark polish matched back to the lip on stage.'

Motherly advice

'My mother would always tell me to moisturise my legs, which is a weird thing. She has always moisturised all over and I have only started to moisturise my face in the last year, which is bad.'

NAOMI WATTS

Beauty musings

'Instead of thinking, "How can I slow the ageing process?" I think, "How can I bend the rules?" Every year you add to your life, you're going to add a different experience to your face. In my forties I keep hydrated with lots of moisturiser and drinking lots of water, and I try to make time for facials.'

Best beauty tip

'I have always coloured [tinted] my lashes and eyebrows as this is good for giving definition to my face.'

Favourite skincare product

'L'Oréal Paris Revitalift Filler.'

Hair

'My hair is very fine so I use volumising shampoo and conditioner. I also take a vitamin called Viviscal and different omegas and fish oils.'

Favourite fragrance

'I tend to be quite subtle with fragrances: I like fresh smells, things you can only really smell close up. I like to change it up as well, sometimes florals, sometimes musky tones. I love anything Dyptique.'

6
HEAD GAMES

*T*WO OF MY FAVOURITE PEOPLE IN THE WORLD are my colourist Damien Rayner and stylist supremo Philip Barwick. They have been patiently tending my locks for over 20 years. In the beauty business I get offers from many fabulous people to cut and colour my hair but, with the very rare exception, I remain loyal to my two trusty men. One notable exception was when I was in Paris and the astonishingly talented Christophe Robin coloured my hair. He is a hair colour god and deeply fabulous person to boot (he colours Kylie Minogue, Claudia Schiffer, Isabelle Adjani, Emmanuelle Béart and Catherine Deneuve's hair, to name just a few).

Christophe's salon is snugly tucked away on the first floor of the hotel Le Meurice, an oasis of cool and comfort. The cutting capes are emblazoned with dragons and the artwork has a distinctly cheeky bent. Christophe worked his magic on my hair to create the perfect vanilla blonde while beguiling me with his naughty charm. This was a serious rockstar moment. Not only did I have fabulous Parisian hair, but I was also introduced to Christophe's hair care products, my favourite being the Regenerating Mask with Rare Prickly Pear Seed Oil. Of course I asked for permission first from Damien, who gave his blessing, as Christophe is his hair colouring hero. It is essential to be open about any hair indiscretions or suffer the hurt of being seen as a betrayer. This is emotional territory, and I asked Damien how he felt if clients broke up with him. 'I used to take it personally, but nowadays, I'm pretty cool with it. I don't want to be stuck in a bad relationship.'

For me, both Phil and Damien have been on the crazy Darling journey, looking after my head both outside and in. Every six weeks I head off for a cut and colour and, invariably, a therapy session. I always sink into the chair with a sense of absolute abandon. This really is the perfect relationship: there is the pampering and the download, and you leave with great-looking hair. I love the blow-dry moment at the end. The warmth from the blow-dryer combined with having my hair played with invariably sends me off to sleep. This rates as one of my top relaxing beauty moments.

Cut and colour are closely aligned, as one predicates the other: depending on who you are talking to, either cut or colour is king. I used to have both done in the one sitting when Damien and Phil worked together. It was deep-breath territory as the colour would take two hours and then Phil would wield his scissors for the next hour. By the end I would be itching to get out of the chair. Now, the two processes are split, which makes for a much more cheerful me. Damien always laughs, saying that after he has coloured my hair, Phil cuts all the good bits off.

From a young age I was quite 'experimental' with my hair. I lived in Roseville and went to a salon in the strip on the Pacific Highway that hasn't changed its hoardings since the 70s. The hairdresser was keen to have a willing experimenter in her midst. I was at Ravenswood School for Girls and the strictures were set in stone, but I proceeded to push the boundaries in spite of the hats and gloves rule. One memorable cut was the 'beret': all short on one side and long on the other. I thought it was so cool. Next came the little blonde duck tail, a small triangle of hair that sat at the base of my natural brunette bob. I was one of the first on the North Shore to have the Vidal Sassoon-inspired 'coupe sauvage'. God, I loved that cut, although it did involve a perm. Now, don't judge me, it was all about the texture. Picture this: hair all shoulder length and layered, then lightly permed to create the perfect shag – very 1975. Trailblazer at all times, though I'm not sure the teachers appreciated how fashion forward it was.

My biggest mistake was loving that look too much. I went back and had it done a second time; my hair did not appreciate the perming process and had a fit of the vapours (I am so back in that 70s moment) that left my hair fried. Lesson learned, and no perming solution has touched my hair since. Although I have heard on the grapevine that perms are on their way back.

Next it was a change of schools, to Barker College in Hornsby. Yes, a boys' school that had just gone co-ed in Year 11 and 12. And with the ratio of two boys to one girl, it was time for a hair update. The perm had finally grown out and I was going through another awkward stage, which reared its head every so often, so I was hiding behind a curtain of sweeping fringe that covered my right eye. The blackout curtain was so effective that I started getting those weird eye floaters dancing across my vision. Definitely time for a new cut, so back to the trusty salon – see, loyalty at all times – and the Cleopatra cut, another hair highlight: shoulder-length with a very blunt fringe. It was then that I embraced the power of the fringe and have basically never looked back.

The beauty of a fringe is you can change it up. I have experimented with the Julius Caesar fringe, so short it was almost non-existent (warning: this must not be attempted after the age of 22, maybe never); the blunt brow-sweeping fringe that worked best for me teamed with the LOB (long bob) and was pitch perfect in the 70s; the all-round fringe, Friar Tuck or pudding-bowl style, that believe it or not I rocked in 1983. This was in another of my growing-out phases, where I said to my stylist that I wanted to grow my hair all one length and not muck around with those highly unsatisfactory growing-out hair cuts that look neither one thing nor the other. So he obliged me, and my hair resembled a circumcised penis; honestly, that is the only way to describe it. It was all one length, grazing the top of my ears, and then the rest was undercut. What was I thinking? But it did kind of work and it did grow out uniformly.

My next hair experiment was in my mid-20s, when I started to play with colour. My hair was then being tended to by a fabulous colourist called Bryan Thompson, who now lives and works in New York, and he took me into the realms of red: a Botticelli-inspired Titian red became my signature colour, teamed with vibrant green contact lenses. My hair was long, all one length, with a blunt fringe and a uniform block of colour; this look saw me through my 20s and into my early 30s. At the height of my red phase, when I was 30, my 'best man' at my wedding, Ian, who I had gone to school with, even referenced my hair in his speech, saying that he was one of the few people there who knew what my true hair colour was.

There are so many red hues to choose from and my personal favourite is Titian with a nod to strawberry blonde. Other enticing colourways come in ginger bread, saffron and terracotta. On a prescriptive note, firebrand reds suit those who are born redheads and those with pale to light-olive complexions, while natural brunettes will always suit rich reds. Those with dark skin should probably steer clear of reds altogether. For me, as the seasons and the sunlight changed, it was a great time to experiment with auburn tones in winter and rose gold in summer. Cheeky highlights of pastel pinks and apricots can create a peekaboo effect, either with permanent colour or a fun fix of wash-out hair chalk like Kevin Murphy's Color Bug.

A S WITH ALL THINGS BEAUTY, maintenance is at the forefront, particularly with red shades, as they are very vulnerable to the effects of UV damage. Red pigment can be tricky and is particularly susceptible to fading. To help maintain the intensity of colour, it is essential to use products specifically designed to conserve colour and then style with a UV protectant.

There are also some general makeup rules that apply when you have red hair, such as using yellow-based foundations to counteract any redness in the skin that will clash with red hair. For eyeshadow, soft chestnut browns and golden shades, which I am obsessed with, work brilliantly teamed with a chocolate-brown eyeliner rather than black. For cheeks and lips, a plum stain works a treat and the finishing touch, a hint of bronzer, will keep skin looking filled with light. Having said all this, I am a great one for breaking as many rules as possible. Hey, if it looks great, just wear it. I remember a phenomenal product that I still have, a Chanel Eye Gloss Quad with exceptional texture and colours, including a glossy white, gold, berry and black. The berry quadrant is the one I adore. It kind of looks as if I have been crying but in a really good way.

The one thing to remember with reds is that it is the hardest pigment to remove from your hair so be very, very sure before you take the leap. I would even go as far as trying on a red wig just to get a feel for how the colour works against your skin. The maintenance regime is demanding and to keep the red looking fresh, I was always visiting the salon midway between appointments for a colour refresher with a gloss or toner for a refreshing boost. If the annoying regrowth stripe is too much in evidence, grab a root concealer to help you limp to your next appointment.

In my very last experimental hair deviation, ever, before I settled down with Phil and Damien, I was working at *Vogue* and the mullet was having a brief resurgence on the catwalk and, you guessed it, I was talked into adopting this rather extreme cut. My hair was shoulder-length and brunette and my fringe began a new life that ended at the top of my ears, complete with an undercut. I convinced myself that my hair looked cool. And then, in an even feebler moment, I allowed the boundaries of good taste to be pushed even further by allowing the colourist to bleach my oversized fringe white-blonde. *What?* I hear you scream. Yes, I looked like a racoon and not in a good way. I froze on the spot but my upbringing prevented me from saying it was the ugliest fringe I had ever seen and could they please dye it back. So I reeled out of the salon and sprinted straight to the chemist.

I sheepishly approached the counter as I had never, ever tried dyeing my hair

In my very last experimental hair deviation, I was working at Vogue and the mullet was having a brief resurgence on the catwalk . . .

at home, and begged for advice. I was helpfully advised that I should have thought twice before experimenting like that at home. *No, lady, I actually paid for this.* Clutching what I hoped would be my saviour, I raced home and clumsily slapped a brunette shade on the offensive stripe. Little did I realise that I would create the perfect shade of khaki. With squinting eyes I convinced myself that it looked fine – that is, until I turned up at work the next day. I ran into someone at an event recently, who thought she remembered me hosting an event in a bath of all things. My mind clouded as said she remembered that I had green hair; I vehemently denied that it was me.

Looking back on it, I really should have had the courage to say that it was an epic fail and could they please fix it. Twenty years down the track and I think I would now be able to do so. Though you just don't know. I have had some woeful blow-dries at times too, where I probably should have asked them to do it again, but have just worn it and wet my hair down at home. It's all about etiquette.

The brunette I was in early 2000 was probably the closest thing to my natural hair colour, so the maintenance was less. It was an all-over permanent colour, which I had recoloured every six weeks with an in-salon gloss treatment mid-way through to take out any brassiness. To keep the brunette shade looking rich, I was told to try not to over-shampoo. This is impossible for me as I wash my hair every day. I have canvassed many hairdressers on the daily wash rule and the reports are mixed. As usual, I winkle out the one that works for me. My hair is fine, but there is lots of it and it's quite oily and I just don't feel clean if I don't. The trick for me is to use a gentle shampoo with a single application, like Aveda Shampure Shampoo (also fabulous for washing cashmere clothing), on the roots only, and try a very light conditioner, Shampure Conditioner, just on the ends. I occasionally push my hair out to two days by using dry shampoo, but to be honest I don't feel a hundred per cent clean. One trick I occasionally use is just shampooing my fringe to give the bulk of my hair a break.

As for blow-drying technique, mine is beyond minimal. I spritz on a heat protectant – one of my favourites is KMS Free Shape Quick Blow Dry – and then whoosh my fringe from side to side with the heat (keeping the dryer 10 centimetres from my hair and constantly moving it to avoid over-heating the cuticle), and a paddle brush and then run a barrel brush through the rest. I have the hair-dryer on a low heat setting and work the air through the roots to create extra volume. As my hair is fine, I go easy on the styling products, with a little root boost to bulk up my hair. But, let's face it, there is nothing as uplifting as having a great blow-dry done by someone else. If I could, I would have my hair blow-dried professionally daily.

I have also discovered the power of the curling iron as a pick-me-up for my mid-length, layered hair. For a going-out trick, I unstrategically work the barrel through my bone-dry hair, having prepped it with a heat protectant. I cannot believe it has taken me all these years to embrace this power tool. The mark of success is when the beauty pack give me a tick for effort.

I also always use a good colour-conserving shampoo with UV filters, as the sun is harsh on all coloured hair. Once a week, I replenish my hair with a deeply moisturising treatment, like the legendary Terax Original Crema, a great all-rounder that can be used as a conditioner to help maintain the moisture levels in the hair or as leave-in 15-minute treatment. To give my locks a boost during the brunette phase, I had a subtle infusion of blonde added to the tips of my hair, with some artfully placed balayage pieces for summer.

This was the catalyst for taking myself blonde, or rather having my colourist do it. Going from brunette to blonde was a serious initial time commitment: six hours in the chair. The thing I love about being blonde is that my colour remains a work in progress. Whenever I arrive to see Damien, every five weeks, the brief is always 'Let's go blonder.' I love the look of freshly coloured hair; the process also swells the hair shaft, which gives you more body and volume. I'll never forget the time I was visiting my mother-in-law in hospital and I had just had my hair coloured. There was a woman in the other bed who asked me if I was my mother-in-law's granddaughter. Amazing what the power of a good haircut and colour can do. I loved this comment; on the other hand my husband, who was also there, was not that impressed as it meant he looked old enough to be my father.

Damien has experimented with all the variations, from high-maintenance, squeaky-clean champagne blonde, which works with my fair complexion, to vanilla, parchment, clotted cream, ash, lavender and beyond. Keeping the blonde fresh and clean and minimising the colour leaching is all about having hair in pristine condition, so I have an in-salon gloss treatment mid-way between colour sessions if I have the time. If not, I do a weekly boost at home, with a champagne- or beige-based coloured shampoo and conditioner, always remaining mindful of the fact that all colour builds up on the hair, so I am careful not to overuse it. I love Goldwell Dualsenses Blondes & Highlights Shampoo and Conditioner, which doesn't overload my hair. I also keep Wella System Professional Repair Mask in the shower for a weekly protein boost, as without protein there is nothing for the colour or moisture to bind with.

My hair grows like weeds, so for three weeks the colour is perfect, but for the last two, the telltale marsupial-grey roots start to creep through. One of my cult finds that helps me traverse this two-week hiatus is a root concealer. The stylist Charles Worthington has perfected his seriously clever Instant Root Concealer, which is a temporary colour spray that covers grey hair and hides root regrowth. My colour of choice: Dark Blonde.

WHEN THINKING ABOUT CHANGING YOUR HAIR COLOUR, it's always good to rely on the experts to give you an honest answer (except when it comes to dyeing your fringe a separate colour to the rest of your hair – see above!) as so much depends on skin colouring and complexion. Get the shade right and your hair colour will make your eye colour pop and help to balance out skin tone issues.

I was at my reading group the other night (we have been a tight team for 24 years), which is a great touchstone for all things beauty related. The crew have witnessed all of my beauty dabblings and experimenting, and we were canvassing the great grey debate. We brought up some sexy greys, including Helen Mirren, Sarah Harris, Kristen McMenamy, Meryl Streep in *The Devil Wears Prada*, George Clooney and my reading group buddy. Really, it's all about attitude and a really good grey. The question is whether to go with the flow and embrace your new-found colour, or fight it all the way. I'm fighting it to the death.

Today, Phil and I have arrived at the perfect fringe. The cut is a little hark back to the coupe sauvage but without the perm factor – so all shaggy, layered and shoulder-length with a fringe that starts out sweeping my lashes. By the time I am back for my six-weekly appointment, my fringe has morphed into a sideswept version: a two-in-one. My beloved fringe is a great beauty asset, as it also hides any overdue forehead Botox. The thing I love about Phil is his consistency – for me he is the master of the no-haircut haircut. He always listens to what I want and is highly simpatico. Sometimes he takes it a little shorter and shaggier, sometimes he leaves the length; it just feels supremely right each time. On a couple of occasions I have attempted to grow the fringe out, but it always ends up looking really flat and I invariably return to my tried and tested fringe.

Both Phil and Damien are trusty confidantes who have always been there for me during the highs and the lows of life. I love this snippet from the *Sassoon ABC Cutting Guide*, which says that the job of a hairdresser is '10 per cent ability and 90 per cent psychology'. With my guys I would say it is 100 per cent of both. For me, sitting in the chair is a chance to download and clear my head, literally and figuratively.

TERMS AND CONDITIONERS

A is for AGEING HAIR

In your 20s your hair is at its best, but once you hit 30, your hair can start to suffer from ageing. If you colour it, heat style it, swim with it or expose it to UV rays, odds on you have damaged and aged it. So unless you want to shave it all off or opt for the 'circumcised penis cut' I mentioned earlier and start again from scratch, the first person to turn to is your stylist for a dedicated prescription. In the quest to address ageing hair, the hairdressing industry has turned to skincare for inspiration. The big guns have come up with an arsenal that targets ageing hair: Kérastase has its Age Premium range and Redken has Cerafill, while K-Pak Revitaluxe Restorative Treatment is good for instant hair repair. For protection from the ravages of UV rays, try Lakme Teknia Sun Care Serum. On the internal front, ensure you have a diet rich in vitamin D, iron, iodine, protein and zinc. Over the age of 40, hair can suffer from hormonal changes; you may notice it getting finer due to shrinking follicles, and there are of course the creeping greys. Be sure to massage your scalp regularly to increase circulation. In your 40s, the trick is to go for volume rather than poker-straight hair, as it is more flattering. 'Straight hair pushes your features forward; volume softens them,' reveals my colourist Damien Rayner. By this stage, hair diameter has thinned and the growth cycle changes. 'More hair follicles are resting, so less hair is actually growing and the rate slows down,' says trichologist Philip Kingsley.

Try to go easy on the high-octane styling, as years of exposure to irons and blow-dryers will have left your hair dried-out and brittle. If you use a hairdryer every day, switch to a cooler setting.

Hair loss and thinning can also be an issue. Each strand of hair usually grows about two and a half centimetres every two months for four years, then fallsout and is replaced by a new one. But in female pattern baldness, which affects up to 40 per cent of women, hair begins to thin on the top of the scalp and sometimes all over the head. The problem is often inherited, but a hormone imbalance can also be a culprit. Try Rogaine for Women to help stimulate new growth. To create extra volume, try Alterna Extra Hold Hair Spray, which has none of the side effects of some hairsprays that can leave hair feeling stiff. For split ends, try Pantene Split End Repair Serum, a leave-in treatment that combats split ends, and for thinning hair try Joico Cliniscalp Advanced Thinning Rescue for intense follicle nourishment.

B is for BLOW-DRY

Needless to say, I love a professional blow-dry, which takes around 30 minutes and can carry me into the next day. If blow-drying at home, work with small sections and a round boar-bristle brush like Moroccanoil's. As with all good beauty routines, the prep is essential. For my fine hair, I would first use a detoxing shampoo and follow with a volumising shampoo, combed through with conditioner in the shower, using the must-have Tangle Teezer, a genius wet or dry detangling hair brush that will change your life and free your hair of knots. Conditioner causes the cuticle on the hair shaft to lie flat so it reflects light, giving you glossier hair. Next comes the heat protectant and again, comb through with the Tangle Teezer for thorough coverage. The fringe comes first, with a blow-dryer on medium heat and intensity, using a small radial brush and brushing from side to side. This part is easy. Next, I rough-dry my hair upside-down to create more volume. Now for the labour-intensive part: hair needs to be dried in four sections, starting with the bottom section, closest to my neck, while the rest is securely clipped to the top of my head. Using a round brush, I begin at the roots and slowly work the brush down my hair, followed closely by the dryer. I repeat this three times, trying to be patient enough to do the same with each section. Let's just say practice makes perfect. Tip: keep brushing, spinning and blow-drying until each section is bone-dry.

C is for COLOUR CONSERVATION

Avoid washing your hair the day after colouring, to let your scalp's natural oils build up. Then invest in a good colour-protecting cleanser and conditioner like Bumble and Bumble Color Minded Shampoo and Conditioner. For ongoing protection, try a heat-activated anti-breakage dynamo like L'Oréal Professional Serie Expert Force Vector Shampoo and Conditioner and, if you are blonde, it's important to use a de-brassifier like O&M TLC Blonde Silver Shampoo. For brunettes try the all-purpose Redken Colour Extend Shampoo and Conditioner. If you need a colour boost but are short on time, the wizards at John Frieda have a 3-minute in-shower gloss treatment called Luminous Color Glaze, which comes in six shades of blonde, brunette and red.

C is also for CURLS

Curly and wavy hair is notorious for behaving itself only until humidity takes hold, and then waves turn to frizz. So wash hair with a small amount of a gentle shampoo such as Matrix Biolage Hydrating Shampoo, then use a light conditioner such as Kérastase Crème Elasto-Curl and run it through the ends. Just pat hair and don't towel dry as this can cause frizz. Abandon the flat iron and blow-dryer and let your hair dry naturally, coiling a few random waves of hair around your finger and then uncoiling them. The less you fiddle with curls, the better they will look. Next, apply a small amount of shine serum, such as Fudge Gloss Dual-Purpose Blow-Dry and Finish Serum, onto your palms and work gently into the ends. But above all, learn to love the texture you were born with.

D is for DAMAGE CONTROL

This category is a biggie. Bleaching or chemically relaxing hair can cause it to become up to 60 per cent weaker. The first line of defence is a targeted shampoo and conditioner, such as Toni & Guy Cleanse Shampoo and Conditioner for Damaged Hair. Try to hold your hairdryer above your head the way your hairdresser does. The hot air will then flow down the cuticle and keep hair looking smooth. To finish off, use your cool-shot control to seal the cuticle. If static electricity is an issue, try running a comb or a boar-and-nylon-bristle brush spritzed with hairspray through your hair. With straightening irons, keep the number of passes over the hair to two at the most, otherwise hair will start to look fried, and apply a minuscule amount of finishing serum to the ends of the hair, as that is where the need is greatest. Humidity can turn even the sleekest locks into a frenzy of flyaways, so look for serums and balms that will tame the beast. Apply Wella SP Ends Express to towel-patted hair, paying particular attention to the ends, and style for a smooth finish. Leave-in conditioners are also a good option, as they retain moisture; try Kèrastase Reflection Lait Chroma Reflect.

Heat protectants protect hair from the onslaught of heated styling tools and are an essential part of the styling arsenal – try ghd Heat Protect Spray.

Chlorine is also one to watch out for as it will damage your hair cuticle and make it brittle, but it is actually the metals in the water (generally copper) that leave a greenish residue on your hair. To get your hair back to its normal colour, you need to restore the pH balance. There are detoxing shampoos and conditioners on the market that are designed specifically for this problem, such as Kérastase Bain Aprés-Soleil Shampoo and Soleil Créme Richesse Masque.

These will cleanse, rehydrate and repair hair that has been exposed to the sun, salt water or chlorine. Or try dissolving a dozen aspirin tablets in warm water and rinsing it through your hair for a quick home remedy.

E is for EXFOLIATION

Here, hair care borrows from skincare. The scalp builds up dead cells that can result in flaking and oiliness, so to help accelerate the scalp's microcirculation, try exfoliating it once a week to clear away any build-up of product and dead skin cells. Before beginning, give your scalp a little massage with your bristle brush to loosen things up, then try Alterna Caviar Exfoliating Scalp Facial with fruit enzymes and microbeads to get rid of the build-up of dead skin cells. Then shampoo and condition as normal.

F is for FRAGRANT HAIR

I love the smell of luxe hair products and the fact that you can step it up a notch with dedicated hair fragrances. The beauty of fragrances that are customised specifically for hair is that they won't dry the hair out, and due to their super-light oil base and the fact that hair is moving all the time, acting as a diffuser, they pervade for a long time. Uber-stylist Serge Normant created his very own delicious hair fragrance with notes of ylang-ylang, jasmine and amber called Avah Eau de Parfum. Also high on the love list is Frédéric Malle Carnal Flower hair mist, a blend of tuberose and musk, and the classic Byredo Bal D'Afrique with intoxicating notes of neroli, marigold and cedarwood.

G is for GREYING

Greys can start sprouting at any time – in fact the median age for the grey alert is 34, although it can be younger – but the 40s are when you start contending with them in earnest, along with changes in hair texture. Be warned against pulling greys out, as this can distort the hair follicle and result in more crinkly hair.

Every hair follicle contains melanocytes, which are pigment cells; when you first start to grey it is because the melanocytes have become less active. As a result, less pigment is deposited into the hair and that makes it appear lighter. As greying progresses, the melanocytes die off until there are no cells left to produce any colour.

OPTION 1 If you love your grey hair, use a silver shampoo to help maintain a shiny and lustrous look. If you have coloured your hair and want to go entirely grey, this is a big undertaking and it can take up to a year to get uniformity. You want a clean rich blue-grey, definitely not marsupial grey.

OPTION 2 If you colour your hair to hide the grey, work with lighter shades and various hues of blonde around the face. This is much less ageing than harsher, darker shades. Invest in a good colourist to help banish the greys. And if you are a fan of home hair colour, L'Oréal Paris have developed a specific home hair-colour range called Excellence Age Perfect to hide greys and add light and shine to hair.

OPTION 3 Masks should be part of your hair care arsenal to keep hair deeply conditioned. As hair ages it is very prone to breakage and sun damage. Add moisture if hair has become unruly and frizzy with Paul Mitchell Instant Moisture Daily Treatment or Matrix Hydra-Seal Softening Mist, and protein if hair has become limp and lifeless with De Lorenzo Essential Treatments Protein Complex.

H is for HOME HAIR COLOUR

For those who have a highly developed fear factor when it comes to home hair colouring including yours truly (remember the khaki incident), there have been meteoric improvements, such as mousses that go on like shampoo and create shimmery, easy-to-wear colour. Try L'Oréal Paris Sublime Mousse or John Frieda Precision Foam Hair Colour. After shampooing hair, wait at least 24 hours before colouring and then select a shade no more than 2 levels away from your existing colour. If you have coloured, straightened or permed (yes, there's that word again) your hair, wait for two weeks before home colouring, and always apply to dry hair.

I is for INNOVATION

Keep your eyes peeled for a peptide formula that mimics hair protein to help restore elasticity and strength to tortured hair. KhairPep has a hair mask and leave-in serum that helps repair damaged hair by helping to increase strength and elasticity.

J is for JENNIFER ANISTON

She still has *the* most desirable hair in the business. She is also part-owner of hair care uber-brand Living Proof. I am a big fan of the hero product, Restore Recovery Regimen, with ampoules that you use once a week for a month instead of conditioner to help recondition very damaged hair.

K is for KERATIN HAIR TREATMENTS

This is a salon-based treatment that creates smooth and tangle-free hair for up to 12 weeks. It is a semi-permanent hair smoothing chemical treatment made up of chemical formaldehyde, conditioners and keratin, kind of the opposite of a perm. Keep straightening treatments down to a couple a year to take the stress off your hair, as every time you do one, your hair becomes more brittle. To keep up the good work use a sulphate-free shampoo and steer clear of 'beach sprays'; these work in the opposite direction and can cause frizz to reappear. There is some controversy over the use of formaldehyde, and you can get straightening treatments that are formaldehyde-free, but they don't last quite as long.

L is for a LOVE AFFAIR WITH LONG HAIR

After the experimental days of my youth I have always embraced long hair. I had a hilarious debate once with a friend, whose hair was only slightly longer than mine, I might add, who insisted that my hair was only medium length, but anyway. Changing it up keeps the look fresh with artfully worked layers or a multi-tasking fringe. As hair guru Oribe says, 'Bangs are the easiest way to reinvent long hair.'

According to stylist Kerry Warn, 'Women love long hair because of its versatility, and men like it because it's so sexy.' Long locks are very vulnerable to heat-styling damage so remember, before you reach for your blow-dryer or hot iron, always apply a heat protectant. Also, a weekly deep-conditioning treatment will help with split ends and the condition of your hair. Protect your hair overnight by applying a leave-in conditioner or split ends serum like Ojon Damage Reverse Instant Restorative Hair Serum and then plaiting it loosely. If you have fried your hair and it's looking damaged and heat-exhausted, take note. Heat is the main cause of hair damage, and too much may cause the water in the hair shaft to overheat, making hair weak and brittle. If you're in need of hair rehab, I recommend a three-pronged approach: head to the salon for a deep-conditioning restorative treatment that is suited to your hair type;

get your hair trimmed to rid it of split ends, which are the telltale signs of damaged hair; and finally, as a cosmetic alternative, use a shine serum to restore a healthy look. Try Sachajuan Shine Serum.

Hair grows about 12 millimetres each month, so tend that mane lovingly to keep it healthy by massaging your scalp regularly to improve blood flow to the hair follicles. Hair is your crowning glory, so don't skimp on product either; invest in a good shampoo and conditioner like Kevin Murphy Luxury Wash and Luxury Rinse, or Evo Day of Grace Leave-in Conditioner, a lightweight conditioner chock-full of proteins and moisturisers to prep and detangle.

M is for MASKS

Leave one in the shower to remind you to use it because if you are like me, it's out of sight, out of mind. They are great applied to the ends as a weekly treatment, as they contain ramped-up ingredients such as butter oils and wax-based conditioners. They are great for long hair, as it is likely old hair with a history of heat styling, chemical processing and sun exposure. For an extra boost, wrap your hair in plastic wrap and apply heat with a blow-dryer to improve absorption of the mask. Protein masks help strengthen hair, while moisturising masks help hydrate it. Three good all-rounders are Davines Nourishing Hair Building Mask, Aesop Rose Hair & Scalp Moisturising Masque and Redken Frizz Dismiss Mask.

N is for the NEVER RULES

- Never put an iron on hair that is not bone-dry and heat-protected. If you see steam or hear sizzling, abort.
- Never drastically change your hairstyle immediately after a break-up.
- Never cut your own hair, ever!

O is for OILS

Hair oils can be used as a pre-shampoo treat for the hair and the scalp, or as a styling aid to create silky-smooth hair and tame flyaways. When taming frizz, remember the golden rule: go lightly, heating a small amount in the palms of your hands first, and lightly run it through the ends of the hair. Try Moroccanoil Light Oil Treatment.

P is for the POWER OF THE PICTURE

Forget a thousand words: in salon land a picture speaks volumes. Inspiration is everywhere. Just think of Rihanna's ever-changing styles; this girl's had more haircuts than hot dinners. Jessica Alba and Gisele Bündchen define warm, biscuit-coloured hair. Abby Lee defines fringes, while Alexis Chung is a trendsetter in both colour and cut. Jennifer Aniston still rocks everything about her hair.

Q is for QUICK FIX

The words dry shampoo immediately spring to mind. My all-time favourite is still Klorane Extra Gentle Oat Milk Dry Shampoo. Whether purse size or full size, you should have one stashed strategically in the bathroom, the glovebox and deskside. No one should be without this product, ever. It gives day-old blow-dries a boost, soaking up oil, and also acts as a fabulous volumiser. The only criticism that could ever be levelled at this cult product in the past was that it favoured blondes because it left a pale residue in the hair, but all hail Klorane for addressing this with their brunette oat offering. Party trick: before going out, tip your head forward and blast your roots with the hairdryer, then tousle through the dry shampoo with your fingertips. Et voilà, va-va-va-voom hair.

R is for REPAIR

We all focus so much on skincare, but it's just as important to keep hair in pristine condition too. Get hair into rehab with a toolkit that targets moisture and strengthening.

- The first rule of thumb when finishing shampooing and conditioning: rinse, rinse and then rinse again to help minimise product build-up in the hair.
- Wash with a gentle shampoo that moisturises without weighing hair down, like **Klorane Gentle Shampoo and Conditioner with Oat Milk**.
- A hair mask rich in antioxidants is helpful for damaged, colour-treated hair; try **Pureology Strength Cure Restorative Masque**.
- As we all know, in Australia we're constantly exposed to the biggest ager in the business, the sun. It affects our skin and hair, so it is vital to apply a UV protector to hair to stave off UV damage. Try **Joico K-Pak Sun Therapy Protective Sun Milk**.
- If your hair is coloured and let's face it, whose isn't, try a colour-saving shampoo and conditioner like **Redken Color Extend Magnetics**.
- Coat the mid-lengths to ends of hair with a hair protector like **ghd Heat Protect** to seal the cuticle and minimise the damage of heat stylers like blow-dryers and hot irons.
- Heat stylers, colouring, brushing and combing all damage the oldest part of the hair, so a product that targets split ends is an essential part of your arsenal. Try **TRESemmé Split Remedy Leave-in Conditioning Spray**, which features polymer technology to temporarily bond the frayed strands back together.

S is for SERUMS AND SHINE SPRAYS

These are often silicone-based, coating the hair shaft to enhance shine and softness. Always apply sparingly, as you don't want to weigh hair down or make it greasy. Don't spray directly onto the hair; instead, spray into the palms of your hands. Then you can distribute the serum evenly. Inecto Pure Citrus Shine Boost Serum can be used either before you blow-dry, to help tame flyaways and frizz, or after, as a finishing product. Or try Kérastase Sérum Thérapiste, with an oil base to moisturise and cream to help seal split ends.

S is also for SHAMPOOS

I had to sneak a second S in. Shampoos are detergent-based and alkaline and clean by lifting the cuticle to remove the dirt. Never use too much shampoo and, for me, I only shampoo once, concentrating on the scalp rather than the ends. Clarifying shampoos should be used once a week to remove any build-up of dirt, styling products, chlorine and salt water. Try KMS Daily Fixx Clarifying Shampoo.

T is for THICKENING

Go for volume at the roots, as high hair flatters everyone. Even straight hair looks more polished with volume at the roots. I remember visiting a stylist once (not Phil) who said, as he stared intently at me in the mirror, that as we age, we need to pump more volume into the hair. I laughed and said that obviously he would be blow-drying my hair poker-straight then. No response. For an instant volume boost, try John Frieda Luxurious Volume Root Booster, applied to either side of the part and blow-dried in, as it creates an instant lift. Must-have tools are a wide-toothed comb or Tangle Teezer, stored in the shower, for combing through conditioner and masks. Brush your hair with a quality brush that won't injure the hair shaft, such as a Mason Pearson or Kiehl's, before shampooing, so your hair is tangle-free to start with. Brushing also helps stimulate blood supply to the hair follicles. Remember to wash brushes at regular intervals with warm soapy water and then leave them to air-dry. For those with naturally thick hair, again brushing will help to stimulate the scalp and distribute natural oils, then shampoo once or twice a week with a moisturising shampoo; try Sebastian Hydre Moisturising Shampoo. Blot hair dry, separate out with a wide-toothed comb and apply a detangling formula, such as Goldwell Moisture Definition Detangler Spray, which will keep hair looking shiny and bouncy. Then dry hair with a diffuser to keep it calm and apply a shine spray to keep it looking smooth. Try tecni.art Gloss Control.

U is for UPDO

For an instant glamour boost, equestrian-inspired chignons that sit tight on the neck with a centre part are a winner. Begin with a centre part and clip apart a five-centimetre section from each side of your head. Take the rest of your hair and create a low ponytail, then twist it up into the base of your neck, pinning it as you go. Then take the two front pieces and pin them into place over the bun. Finish with a glossing spray.

V is for the GODFATHER OF CUTTING, VIDAL SASSOON

His revolutionary, precision-cut 60s bobs that often had an asymmetrical twist (see, I was on to something in the 70s) broke all the hair rules. Sassoon stated: 'To me, hair meant geometry, angles, cutting uneven shapes as long as it suited that face and that bone structure.' His tagline was, 'If you don't look good, we don't look good.'

W is for WAVES

Bring on the ripple effect. To give hair a break from all that heat styling, try air-drying instead, using a hydrating mousse or a hair oil like Shu Uemura Art of Hair Essence Absolue Nourishing Protective Oil. Apply to clean, damp hair and let nature take its course. A great trick for creating relaxed, textured waves is to wash your hair and apply Shu Uemura Art of Hair Wonder Worker Air Dry / Blow Dry Perfector, then plait damp hair into four braids, twist them, clip them up on to your head and then sleep on them. Wake up to great, beachy waves.

X is for X-TREME COLOUR

Take a temporary lead from the locks of music divas like Lady Gaga, Katy Perry, Nicki Minaj and Rihanna and play around with wild colour. Even if is just a hint of gold, apricot or pink, it's fun to experiment temporarily. There are lots of options to play with, including the Kevin Murphy Color. Bug. I love the gold one for dip-dyed hair that wipes on and washes out. Or Fudge's Paintbox, a semi-permanent colour that washes out over time.

Y is for YOLKS

A team of scientists think they might have discovered the secret to unboiling an egg by untangling the proteins that are mixed together when an egg gets cooked. Imagine the impact that would have if it could be translated to the proteins in hair. It could be the great 'protein unscrambler', influencing how hair bends. On a simpler level, if you are caught without any access to a hair mask, eggs contain lecithin and protein to help moisturise hair.

Z IS FOR ZZZZZ NIGHT REPAIR

Try painting Kérastase Nutritive Masquintense on lightly and then
rinse out the next morning; love a product that works while you sleep.
Zinc deficiency has been linked to hair loss, so up your intake with quinoa,
buckwheat and black beans.

I know this is all about me, but I continually struggle with the fear that I may be overwashing my hair. So here's the rub: I have fine oily hair, but the saving grace is there's lots of it. Because it's oily, I have been washing it pretty much every day since I was 13. I have been told on many occasions, by stylists I trust, that it's fine to do this as long as I just foam up at the roots and run my hands lightly over the ends, but sometimes I wonder if they are pandering to me and telling me what I want to hear.

Just the other day I was with someone new (only for a blow-dry!) who said I should wash my hair less to cut down on colour fade as coloured hair is like a 'fine silk shirt'. If you overwash it the colour will fade and look drab and dehydrated, as overwashing strips out colour and moisture. His suggestion: embrace dry shampoo and, if currently washing every day, go to washing every other day.

I have added this to other tricks I have been taught over the years like 'just wash your fringe' or 'rinse your hair without shampooing' or 'just apply conditioner and rinse out'. I have tried all of these for a while – okay, a day – but when it comes down to it I don't feel clean unless my hair is washed daily.

Some facts: sebum (oil) is constantly secreted into the hair and it does build up without washing, and so do styling products. This can all add up to drab, weighed-down hair. Now I love dry shampoo, which binds to the oil and pulls it away from the scalp, but at the end of the day the grime is still there in your hair. That means using dry shampoo day after day rather than shampooing can cause follicles to block and may lead to inflammation, not to mention stinky hair.

HEAD GAMES

EXTREME SPORTS: HOW FAR WILL I GO?

*I*HAVE BEEN IN THE BEAUTY BUSINESS for an exceedingly long time and have seen three decades come and go; things have changed dramatically in that time. I loved the 80s, they were times of excess on so many levels. The industry was awash with money that was spent on astounding events. It was the time when Kerry Packer sold the Nine Network to Alan Bond for the record price of $1.05 billion in 1987, then bought it back three years later for $250 million – a fraction of the original price. At the time I was working as beauty editor on *Mode* magazine and I was also an occasional social reporter.

There was a period when I was flying up to Queensland every week to cover myriad hotel openings related to what became known as the 'white shoe brigade': Queensland moguls who had made their money in a hurry on the property market. One of the most memorable events was the opening of Christopher Skase's new bonanza hotel, the Marina Mirage in Port Douglas, in 1988. It was located on pristine Four Mile Beach, close to the Great Barrier Reef and the Daintree Rainforest. This was five-star on acid. Skase and his company Qintex were worth $1.5 billion at the time and his resorts reflected this largesse. He was famous for splashing his money around, including dispatching his private jet to fly from Port Douglas to Melbourne to pick up a dress for his wife Pixie. We were there for three days, which entailed about two hours of bona fide work: me taking the names of punters as the

EXTREME
SPORTS: HOW
FAR WILL I GO?

photographer worked the room and then writing a paragraph for the social pages.

There were some up-close and personal encounters, as always. I was swimming in the newly minted pool when Christopher Skase suddenly emerged from the bottom wearing snorkelling gear; he was checking on the pool finishes. The hotel went on to become a magnet for celebrities, including Tom Hanks, Mick Jagger, John Travolta and Claudia Schiffer.

The most fun I had (that was vaguely legal) was working on *Mode*'s infamous 'In and Out' list, which pushed the boundaries of every level of etiquette. This was the era of excess and the power lunch was in full swing. The etiquette of the day required you to start lunch at 1 p.m. and most probably not return. Mobile phones were rare, so the bad manners associated with today's usage was non-existent. We talked face to face; life was much less pacey and we still managed to put out a monthly magazine. Fax machines were in full swing and email was a thing of the future. I am always carbon dating myself; I remember, about ten years ago, I was at a function and a colleague was texting furiously while a function presentation was going on. How rude I thought but, now, I am guilty of exactly the same thing. Working as a freelancer, my whole life centres around my mobile. I try to adhere to the old ways and my philosophy of making eye contact at all times, but the lure of the mobile sometimes gets in the way. This is another nail in the coffin of manners.

Up until I finished work at *Madison* in 2013, I didn't have a smartphone I could use to check email. Even on work trips this was no hindrance; it would all be there, waiting for me on my return home. Now, even when on holiday, answering emails is obligatory. I am the first to whip out my phone at the table, and occasionally I even flout my own rules by answering emails during presentations. Who am I? I think I may even suffer from 'nomophobia': fear of being without my mobile phone.

*A*S WELL AS WRITING ABOUT HOTELS, I visited a lot of spas in the course of my work. Navigating the vagaries of the spa world can also throw up some surprises. I encountered an extremely dodgy masseur in Italy who overstepped the mark in the most outrageous way. My husband and I were staying at the 1870 Grand Hotel & La Pace in Montecatini Terme in July 1999. The hotel has a long and illustrious history with guests including Giacomo Puccini, Arturo Toscanini, the former Duke of Windsor and Wallis Simpson, Clark Gable and, now, the Darlings. The hotel is in the heart of the Montecatini wellness spas, famous for their healing waters. On this visit it was full of rich elderly Americans, who were totally at home under the vast ceilings and chandeliers, surrounded by magnificent parquet floors. And so were we.

I was there to test-drive the spa in the hotel and, at 240 euros for a massage, my expectations were high. My husband had tootled off to explore and I headed down to the spa. My therapist was a man who instructed me to get completely undressed as he ran me an algae bath. Now, I am no prude, and in Europe they are much more relaxed about nudity than in Australia, where it's all about the disposable undies, so I tried to be cool and go with the flow. After all, I was staying in a five-star establishment.

EXTREME SPORTS: HOW FAR WILL I GO?

He then invited me to hop into the bath. Okay, fine. But when it was time to get out he began to towel me down, which was the beginning of a spiralling awkwardness. I thanked him, but took the towel from him and dried myself off. Next, I rested on my back covered in the towel for ten minutes. Then the masseur came back, removed my protective towel and started the massage. He pummelled my legs, working his way up my body, proceeding to massage my inner thighs with his face so perilously close to my pubic area that he practically gave me beard rash.

I was very freaked out but wondered to myself if I was being prudish. Maybe this was the Italian way. He was right on the precipice: great beads of sweat were dripping off him on to me and every time I thought I would scream out in protest he seemed to sense this and pull back. Why on earth didn't I get up? At one point he put my foot on his neck. He kept telling me to relax – impossible. This was all being carried out under the guise of a cellulite massage. As I write this, I cannot believe that I subjected myself to this torture. Please don't judge me; it was a weird combination of being on assignment and not knowing if this was how every massage was carried out.

I was screaming on the inside and should have been doing that on the outside. Finally the massage ground to a close. I was a nervous wreck. The worst part is that I had managed to convince myself that I must have been overreacting, until I was on my way out and an ancient wheelchair-bound man turned up for his treatment and the masseur refused to treat him. What! Oh, and before I managed to escape he also asked whether I would like to have another treatment at his home. Er, no!

*W*HAT TO DO? Maybe this is the way they treat cellulite in this town, I thought. (By the way, I didn't even have much cellulite at the time I just hasten to add. Beauty note: if you want to improve the appearance of cellulite, make sure you exfoliate the trouble spots with a good salt scrub like Waterlily Morrocan Melt Sugar Smoother, massaging vigorously and then rinsing it off in the shower. Next, apply either a wash off cosmetic tan like Prtty Peaushun or a fake tan. My new hot favourite is St Tropez Gradual Tan in Shower.) I sprinted out of there, but never made a complaint.

On a completely different tack, when I was on assignment for *Harper's Bazaar* back in 2002, I tackled the 'take it all off' option with the trending bikini-friendly Brazilian wax. There were a number of options on offer at the time: the Hitler-like moustache, parallel runway strips, the mohawk, heart shapes, lightning bolts, initials and the all off. I decided that in order to write the piece effectively, I needed to go directly to the source: Melanie Pavone from Votre Beauté, located deep in the heartland of Double Bay. This, you could say, was the beginning of my career as a bona fide road-tester. How could I write about procedures unless I had actually experienced them first-hand? This tenet is now the lynchpin of my weekly column in *Sunday Life*. One of the beauty lessons I have learnt on the job is that the most effective treatments often involve an element of pain.

The venue was a little startling: a homey apartment complete with pet guinea pig. Rather appropriately, or inappropriately, 'Love Me Tender' was playing as background music. I was new to the 'all off' and as I hopped up onto the bed, Melanie told me to take my underwear off. When I first met her she had been in the waxing game for 18 years.

*EXTREME
SPORTS: HOW
FAR WILL I GO?*

Technique is everything and Melanie was a pro. Her wax of choice was heated beeswax and she was extremely thorough in her quest for the clean-as-a-whistle feel.

The one deeply disconcerting element of my first all off was Melanie's pet guinea pig, who was not feeling well. I'm not surprised, if he was subjected to this porn-meets-torture-show on an hourly basis. He sat shivering on a high stool, watching Melanie's every move. Brave boy.

Post wax, I felt light as air and breezy. I loved Melanie's parting comment. She said: 'It's like when you go scuba diving: the last thing you want to come across is seaweed – all the diver wants to find is the oyster and the pearl.' I was in a car wash years later and got talking to a couple who were also waiting for their car to emerge from the depths of the wash flaps. When they asked what I did for a living, I told them and they were very excited to have met the author of this very story. The wife had read it and immediately beetled off to try the all off for herself. Ah, the power of the press.

Recently, I was sharing some waxing tales with a group of friends, one of whom had just started dating a much younger man. In anticipation of having sex with him she'd had the Hollywood (aka the all off) treatment and was completely free of pubic hair. On the night of the great reveal he was dismayed by the discovery, as he had been excited about the prospect of an older women with the full 'bush'. Funny how fashions change.

After experimenting with the all off over a number of years, I decided to let everything grow back and then neaten the area up with permanent laser hair removal. You need to be very specific about the shape you want and trust your practitioner. I wanted to look like a grown woman but also to have the area looking neat with no knicker overhang. We settled on a small, neat triangle so there would be no fear factor when putting on swimmers.

As we are getting personal, I can't sing the praises of Intense Pulsed Light permanent hair removal highly enough. As with all things, it is very important to have a skilled operator. Even though cost of the initial ten-treatment outlay may seem on the high side, on a cost-per-wear basis it works out to be practically free. I now have no underarm or leg hair and a very tame bikini line. For me it really is a no-brainer. For any strays that re-emerge I have an at-home Philips Intense Pulsed Laser device. It was expensive but it does a great tidy-up job. Just be aware that the technology works best on colour contrast, so unfortunately those with black skin and black hair, or fair skin and fair hair, are not great candidates.

All this talk of hair removal reminds me of the first time I shaved my legs, when I was around 12. I was sitting watching *The Brady Bunch*, quietly admiring my handiwork, when my mother took my breath away by asking me why my legs were so shiny. Sprung. What is it with the rite of passage and the secrecy that surrounds these things? Weird – I guess it's parents not wanting their kids to grow up. With sons it's a much easier process. The only thing I miss about shaving my legs is the delicious feeling of freshly shaved legs rubbing against the sheets when you hop into bed. The thing I don't miss is the gouged skin flaps on my ankles as a result of a careless flick of the blade.

To get a close shave, exfoliate first and then run your razor under hot water to prep it. Next, apply shaving cream and then shave

EXTREME SPORTS: HOW FAR WILL I GO?

against the hair growth with long, even strokes. Finish with a good moisturising body cream like Kiehl's Crème de Corps.

When having any sort of pubic hair removal, you need to leave any self-consciousness at the door. Take some baby wipes for a quick freshen-up before the reveal and be prepared to have your legs splayed out. Take a painkiller half an hour beforehand to take the edge off and remember to breathe. For any ingrown hairs keep a tube of Lucas Paw Paw Ointment at the ready. If the ingrown refuses to budge, it's time to bring out the tweezers. As with all things in life you get what you pay for, so invest in a good pair. I rate Rubis and Tweezerman because they are sharp with a slanted edge. First, exfoliate and dry the affected skin. Grab the tweezers and free up the follicle by scraping away the dead skin. Then pluck. So satisfying.

Fashions do change, so keep this in mind if you are thinking of permanent hair removal. In terms of time, waxing lasts two to four weeks and the triangle (a basic neaten-up) takes about five minutes, the Brazilian takes 15 minutes and the Hollywood, or 'all off', takes 20 minutes.

ONE OF THE BEST RECOVERY RETREATS I have ever been to is Gwinganna Health Retreat. For as long as I have been in beauty, I have wanted to visit this mystical spa retreat, located at Tallebudgera Valley in the luscious hinterland of Queensland's Gold Coast. Those who have gone before me swear by it as a deeply cathartic experience.

Finally, I managed to secure a three-day booking and be inducted into the pure ways of the retreat: no alcohol, no devices, early to bed, early to rise, fresh food, yoga, Nia dance therapy (a low-impact style of dance cardio created in the early 80s), where we leapt around the pavilion in a combination of aerobics and dance that was such an adrenalin rush. I became fixated with the instructor's extreme bell-bottom work-out pants and immediately ordered a pair once I got home and had access to the internet again. Flotation therapy and a series of deeply fabulous treatments including Rockupuncture were on offer. I drank the Kool Aid willingly and have become a devotee of the Gwinganna way.

*E*VERY FUNCTION, LUNCH, INTERVIEW, PRESS TRIP and test drive brings something new and I am always on the lookout for new and sometimes crazy things. I am always putting my body on the line for my beloved reader. But there is one thing I have always shied away from, and that is colonic irrigation. Ever since I heard the tale of a friend who regularly heads off to Thailand for self-administered colonics, I made a promise to myself not to walk that line.

But eventually I was talked into trying my first and, might I add, last colonic. Learning that you store a ridiculous number of kilos of faecal matter in your colon spurred me on to give it a try. The technique I was having was called a closed-system colonic, so nozzles and hoses are all disposed of after use. This is how it works: a small, disposable tube is inserted into the rectum and filtered water fills the colon.

I was on the edge of anxious before we started and my therapist didn't really win my confidence when she announced that her main skill

EXTREME
SPORTS: HOW
FAR WILL I GO?

was naturopathy but that her boss thought she should get some more practice by performing more colonic irrigations. She was basically a novice, like me. *Are you kidding?* I thought. *What part of acceptable is this?* Beauty director, novice colonic operator, review? It did not bode well.

She began by talking herself through the process as she was inserting the anal tube. The words 'Tell me when you feel full' filled me with dread. How am I supposed to judge what full means? Will my bowel explode if I get it wrong?

The water is supposed to 'hydrate' the colon and stimulate the body's own peristaltic action, encouraging the colon to empty itself. This is aided by a reverse vacuum process. At the same time, my therapist massaged my stomach with peppermint oil to encourage evacuation. Her continuous checking of the machine and my failure to produce any backwash 'product' meant things went south pretty quickly. She tried filling and vacuuming three times with absolutely no result and then told me there could be an air blockage (aka fart) that could be interfering with the process. By this stage, with no 'result', I lost heart and ventured that perhaps my system was super-efficient and waste free? And maybe I'm not full of shit after all. About halfway through, I had to call it a day. In my usual submissive way I said I felt that I had let her down.

Personally, I think you should leave the bowel to perform its natural function. Some of the risks of colonic irrigation or colonic hydrotherapy can include a perforated bowel, electrolyte imbalances, abdominal cramping, diarrhoea, nausea and vomiting. For me, I am not going there again.

Having said this, I was convinced to do a series of three consecutive enema treatments combined with fabulous body massage and exfoliation as part of a detox treatments to loosen up 'deep-seated toxins'. Somehow this was different. They used to do enemas on our mothers before they were in full-blown labour in the 6os, so they must be safe, right?

My personalised enemas were oil-and-herb-based. The first, I held on to for roughly five minutes before excreting. Next day was the same process, except this time it was a more intense herbal liquid enema that filled me up. Then it was no-holds-barred: clear the room, it was time for evacuation. Day three was for 'revitalisation and balance' and the final incarnation, another, smaller oil enema. After each treatment I felt pretty trippy and two days later I was bouncing off the walls with the most astonishing energy levels, feeling more productive than I had in years. Two weeks later I was still in the power zone and my skin was really clear. It was hilarious the way people reacted when I shared the information. One friend of mine said that she couldn't bring herself to read the review because it was so graphic. I have done so many treatments and a lot of them have touched a chord, inspiring many readers to front up and put their bodies and faces on the line in the quest for eternal youth.

Some treatments seem a bit out there for the uninitiated, and one treatment that has great results but garnered mixed responses is the 'vampire facial', where your blood is taken, the plasma is filtered and then reinjected into your face. Some seem to find this concept a little confronting. I say embrace it; it's your own DNA. As experimental as I am with my treatments, for me it is really all about trust. I think I have a pretty good radar for the difference between extreme and dangerous. Fingers crossed, to date it has all gone my way.

EXTREME SPORTS: HOW FAR WILL I GO?

SPA RULES TO LIVE BY

- In the spa, turn off your mobile or put it on flight mode. I have made the fatal mistake of having my phone on silent, only to find I can still hear the little sucker vibrating away noisily to itself.

- Get there 15 minutes early just to factor in paperwork and changing. You don't want to eat into your hands-on time.

- If you have had a steam or swim beforehand, jump under the shower for an extra freshen-up and to wash off any chlorine or pool chemicals, as you don't want those being massaged into your skin.

- Be vocal about what you want or don't like (not like me); massage therapists are trained to respect boundaries and they should use draping techniques to make sure you don't feel overexposed.

- Massage pressure can be an issue too, so make it clear from the get-go what you want. I am a weakling and like my pressure medium to light.

- If you are having two treatments, make sure you get the order right. For instance, have your massage before your facial and a body treatment before your massage.

- When the treatment is over, take your time getting up, but not too much time as the next appointment is probably waiting. It's a question of etiquette.

- For me, I like the therapist to be in the room at all times. I think I might have a touch of claustrophobia as well as abandonment issues and have had some anxious-making moments where I have been encased in a body wrap and bound in a space blanket, unable to move, then left for what seems like hours. Every good therapist knows not to leave the room and to give reassuring touches. For me this is critical.

- If you are at a hair salon, the choice of burying your nose in a magazine or being on your phone retrieving emails and checking social media or engaging in scintillating conversation is really up to you. Your trusty stylist will probably be more than happy if you just want to zone out. Being a stylist or therapist all day long must be draining. I have heard confessions from colourists and stylists over the years who say when they get home they apply the 'silence is golden' rule for at least an hour so that they can come back down to earth.
- Personal recommendations are always best. Track down those with great hair, nails and skin and ask them what salons they frequent.
- If it's time to break up with your hairdresser because the relationship has run its course and you feel like changing it up, it's probably best to change salons completely. But, if you are beguiled by a stylist at the same salon and want to make the switch, there is a protocol to toughing it out. Never pretend not to see your former stylist. This rule applies in the big wide world as well. If they ask you who you're seeing, just say that you felt like a change.
- This may seem a bit nit picky, but why are some salon mirrors so unflattering? Surely you just need your head and shoulders in view, not the never-flattering vision of a seated tummy. Bring on the cape at all times.

*EXTREME
SPORTS: HOW
FAR WILL I GO?*

8

BEAUTY KNOW-HOW

AS I HAVE TRAVERSED THE BEAUTY ROAD MAP from my early 20s to my mid-50s, I have realised that you can't change your genetic makeup, but it's never too late to maximise the assets you have. I am always on a learning curve and every day brings new insights. Over my years of being blissfully immersed in beauty I have absorbed, sponge-like, tips and tricks from all corners of the beauty globe and luckily they have stuck with me.

I am famous for never saying 'No' to an invitation. Invariably, every time I interview a beauty expert, have a treatment or attend a beauty function, I pick up some salient new tips. It never ceases to amaze me how much new knowledge there is still to be gleaned.

Read on for the best insider tips and tricks I have harvested over the years, relating to everything beauty from your 20s to your 60s and beyond.

BEAUTY
KNOW-
HOW

THE BEAUTY DRILL

DAILY Cleanse every morning (this is when I do the double cleanse by applying a cleansing oil and then a cleansing balm before I get into the shower) and night with an oil and cleansing cream, using a terry-towel washer or muslin cloth to take it off. This has a twofold action: it removes the day's grime and exfoliates dead skin cells. Make sure to massage the cleanser in firmly and include your neck and décolletage (remember your face ends at your boobs). If your eye makeup is particularly stubborn, use a cottonwool pad soaked in eye makeup remover. Make sure to use a fresh pad on each eye and follow with cleanser.

SERUMS These treat everything under the sun: dehydration, pigmentation, enlarged pores and dullness – and they're famous for their quick penetration. They should be used morning and night. In the morning, use a hydrating serum to plump up your skin and prepare for applying foundation and at night, try an anti-ageing serum to target dullness. Again, firmly massage a few drops all over, including the eye area and neck.

MOISTURISERS I love morning moisturisers that include SPF50. I can't get enough of two-in-one anything. Apply after your serum and make sure to take the cream right around your entire neck. At night, it's the same deal: cleanse, add serum and a dedicated night cream that will leave your skin feeling soothed and plumper when you wake. For a boost, add in a few drops of rosehip facial oil.

EYE CREAM Pat it gently around the orbital bone with your ring finger.

LIP BALM Lips can tend towards dryness and peeling (mine are chronic), particularly as the seasons change. Keep a balm like Hourglass Lip Oil beside your bed to apply morning and night.

ONCE A WEEK Exfoliate, at night, using an AHA (good for anti-ageing and treating fine lines, enlarged pores and dullness) or BHA (good for blemish-prone skins) liquid exfoliator. Try to mask up once a week and also when you fly; try Société Rejuvenating Peptide Gel Masks for super hydration.

SKINCARE THROUGH THE DECADES

SKINCARE IN YOUR TWENTIES

This is the time when your skin is at its peak. Hormones are pumping, and this in turn stimulates sebum, helping to keep the skin hydrated and protected. Of course there is always a flip side: an excess of sebum may cause some breakouts. Everything else, though, is working like a dream: the skin's cell turnover rate is very efficient, at approximately every 14–25 days, which in turn keeps skin looking plump and radiant. I so wish I had appreciated this more at the time.

Establishing a good skincare routine early on is the best way to prevent skin problems later. Get into a habit-forming rhythm by cleansing twice a day and exfoliating once or twice a week with exfoliators containing either AHAs (alpha hydroxy acids) or BHAs (beta hydroxy acids). These ingredients sink into the pores and help dissolve blockages and enhance natural cell exfoliation. Clay masks will help to deep cleanse once a week, and if excess oil is a problem, regular use of a vitamin A moisturiser used only at night will help to slow the over-production of oil. Daily moisturisers should be lightweight and always have an SPF50+ to protect the skin against damaging UVA and UVB rays.

A morning skincare routine should follow these simple steps: cleanser, serum, eye serum, lip protector and moisturiser with SPF50+. And this is where I hop on my very high horse and hit you with my anti-ageing and skin-saving mantra, as even though it won't be visible yet, your skin will probably have received 80 per cent of its long-term sun damage, due to the sun exposure you received before the age of 18.

It is critical that you apply sunscreen SPF50+ to your face, neck and décolletage (in the beauty world, your face ends at your boobs, so treat

this entire area with TLC) and also to the back of your hands, to minimise the intensely ageing damage that is caused by the sun's UVA and UVB rays. On a vanity level this is imperative as an anti-ageing device, but also for health reasons, to try to avoid skin cancer.

I remember hours of fun after sunbaking at Bilgola Beach, peeling layers of skin off my burnt shoulders. Sure enough, in my 30s my first basal cell carcinoma (BCC) popped up on those very same shoulders. It looked like an unresolved pimple, so of course I attempted to extract it myself, not knowing what it was. When I went to have it removed, my plastic surgeon cheerfully informed me, as he was slicing a massive cone of skin out of my back, that I'd had a skin cancer now and was sure to have a few more in the future. Great, something extra to worry about. He left the room at one point and I made the fatal mistake of hopping off the bed to examine the excised tissue. It made me gag. There was a large cone of my flesh, suspended in preservative and waiting to go off to pathology.

Fortunately, I always protected my face in my youth, so it is in quite good nick, but I have a check-up with my beloved dermatologist, Chris Kearney, every six months to keep an eye on the rest of the damage. Sure enough, four years ago another BCC cropped up on my chest. He did such a good job removing it that I can't even see where the little sucker was, though.

Ask any skin expert what their best anti-ageing tip is and wearing a high SPF sunscreen every day will be it. Helena Rubenstein summed it up perfectly when she said that sunburn is like beauty suicide. There are so many amazing products with an SPF component now that all those old whinges about sunscreen being too clogging and thick have gone out the window. At the risk of sounding dogmatic, there is no reason in the world not to wear an SPF every day of the year, and every reason to do so.

ARSENAL

- To target congested skin, try **Neutrogena Skin Clearing Blackhead Cleanser** with salicylic acid.
- Try **MD Formulations Vit-A-Plus Night Recovery**. A dual-action gel moisturiser that helps problem skin by sloughing away dead surface cells.
- For a deep moisturiser, try **Lancôme Visionnaire Nuit Beauty Sleep Perfector**, which works its magic while you sleep.
- For a great sun-protecting tinted moisturiser try **Cetaphil Suntivity SPF50+**.
- For a great all-rounder in the cleansing department, try **DermaQuest Universal Cleansing Oil**.
- Once a week take time out to apply a deep cleansing mask like **Chanel Purifying Cream Mask** with Kaolin and Silica powders to help refine and clarify the skin.
- You know how I love a sunscreen, so I think you should have them scattered everywhere. Some favourites include **Aspect High Protection Sunscreen Lotion** or **Actinica Sunscreen and Ultraceuticals SPF50+** moisturiser.
- To keep hands free of age spots try **Clarins Age-Control Hand Lotion SPF15**.
- **Aspect Vitamin B Serum** gives skin a great boost.
- Gadgets are great if they encourage good cleansing routines; **Clarisonic** has a great range of automatic cleansing brushes that even includes a pedi brush.

THIRTY-PLUS SKIN

This is paydirt time: your body is under more stress than ever before as you juggle work, a partner or a family and often all three. Combine increased stress levels with the demon dehydration (not enough water and too much coffee and alcohol, if you are anything like I was in my 30s), air conditioning and lack of sleep, and this can result in drier, more sensitive skin. You've still got natural radiance, even skin tone and firmness on your side, though, and providing you have used sunscreen regularly, you should have very few deep lines.

If you have neglected to wear sunscreen, fine expression lines and pigmentation will be more likely from sun damage you've incurred in your youth. Cell turnover also starts to slow down to around every 30 days, so skin texture may become duller. Focusing on exfoliation, using an AHA or BHA cleanser, at-home peels or in-salon micro-dermabrasion treatments can help with this. To combat dehydration, try a serum containing rosehip oil like Dr Sebagh Rose de Vie. Also on the menu is an active eye cream and a hydrating lip balm.

ARSENAL

- **Idebenone Facial Cleanser**, which contains AHAs and BHAs as well as a potent antioxidant, idebenone, to help clarify skin.
- **Ultraceuticals Protective Daily Moisturiser SPF50**, a broad-spectrum sunscreen with antioxidants for daily protection.
- **Cosmedix Eye Genius**, which is just that.
- Vitamin C and B serums are essential – try **Aspect C Serum** and **Multi B Plus Serum**. To save on time, dispense a dollop of each onto the back of your hand, combine and apply.

BEAUTY KNOW-HOW

- For lips, try **PCA Skin Ideal Complex Revitalizing Eye Gel**.
- The all-important night step is a retinol-based one. Try **Ultraceuticals Ultimate A+ Anti-Ageing Serum**.

FORTY-SOMETHING SKIN

If you are a masochist and want a little insight into how you will age, take a mirror and place it on a flat surface and look down into it. This will give you a forecast of how gravity will age your face. Ageing affects skin cells' ability to produce collagen and, as a result, skin starts to sag, losing volume and radiance. As we all know, the only acceptable use of the word 'plump' is in reference to the face, and it's an unfortunate fact that as we age it does become a question of 'the fanny or the face': too thin and your face loses volume, which is ageing.

One of the first telltale signs of ageing is droopy upper eyelids; this tends to narrow the eye and give it a hooded appearance. Also, the things that started to manifest in your 30s – facial lines, crow's-feet, vertical lines between the brows, marionette lines that run from the corner of the nose to the mouth – get more pronounced in your 40s unless you have availed yourself of Botox and fillers.

How dramatic these ageing changes are depends largely on genetics, sun damage (the greatest age accelerator in the business) and smoking. At least you have control of two out of three of these factors. With sun damage, UV light breaks down collagen and elastin and can also alter the DNA of cells in the basal layer of the skin. Basically, this accelerates skin's ageing and increases the risk of all types of skin cancer. So, if you do nothing else in your daily anti-ageing regime, you must wear a broad-spectrum sunscreen with an SPF of at least 50 every day on your face, décolletage and the back of your hands. It is never too late to start, but obviously the earlier you adopt this routine, the better your skin will be.

ARSENAL

- Take special care of the delicate skin around the eyes with an age-targeted eye cream. Try **Estée Lauder Resilience Lift Extreme Ultra Firming Eye Cream**.
- Dehydration can become an issue, so try **Société Skin Hydration Complex**, morning and night.
- **Cosmedix Series Protect SPF30+** is a 'physical' sunscreen which blocks all the sun's harmful rays (UVA, UVB and UVC).
- **Tracie Martyn Enzyme Exfoliant**. Use it once a week to slough away dead skin cells and watch it work its wonders.
- Use a retinol-based night cream too. **Diorskin Sculpt** is a good option.

FOREVER-YOUNG FIFTY-PLUS SKIN

It's time for the big guns and a skincare prescription overhaul. The principles for the 50s generally follows the same rules as the 40s but there are some dial-up changes as anti-ageing requires a higher concentration of ingredients. Consulting the experts is always best and I am always on the lookout for fresh new updates from my friends in the business.

One of my favourite cosmetic anti-agers and general mood booster is the expertly applied fake tan. This is my essential holiday starter as I immediately feel slimmer and guilt-free, as I have gained all the benefits of a tan without any of the damage.

BEAUTY KNOW-HOW

For an all-over even fake tan, start exfoliating your body the week before with a body scrub, loofah or buffing cloth to remove dead skin, which can cause the tan to go on unevenly, paying particular attention to dry spots such as knees, elbows and heels. After exfoliating, apply body cream, except on the day of the fake tanning session. If you need to shave or wax, do it a day before tanning, as your skin will be sensitive afterwards and you don't want to irritate it. On the day of tanning, exfoliate but do not apply any moisturiser, perfume, deodorant or makeup.

I prefer to tan in the buff (too much information, I know) to avoid any tan marks.

After you apply the tan, wear loose dark clothing, no bra and open-toed shoes. I repeatedly forget to do this but to date I have not had any streaking on my body. Wait six hours to wash it off, and try applying it in the evening, which allows your body heat to activate the tan while you sleep. Basically, the longer the wait, the deeper the result. Sleep on a towel to avoid tanning your sheets. My favourite products include anything made by St. Tropez.

For best results, pat skin dry after showering, and make sure to moisturise with a moisturiser that does not contain AHAs, as these will hasten exfoliation. Do not exfoliate until you are ready to remove the tan, which should last from five to seven days, depending on your skin type. If you need to touch up, try Glow All Over Spray-on ModelCo Tan in A Can.

For emergency removal, the following will help: soaking in a hot bath then exfoliating in the shower; lemon juice; loofahing; a sugar scrub or having a professional body exfoliation.

No time to fake tan? Slather on gradual tanner as you would a body moisturiser after you shower, as it's easy to apply and develops gradually, or use body makeup or wash-off tan to give your legs a boost. The Body Shop and M.A.C do good versions.

ARSENAL

Follow the same routine as you did in your 40s but here are some added extras:

- I love a cleansing balm: **Elemis** and **Eve Lom** are favourites.
- A pre-cleansing oil, like **Dermalogica**'s, is also great if you have the time.
- Use a moisturiser with SPF50 + and antioxidants – try **Actinica**.
- For exfoliation, Dermalogica do a great gentle rice-based version called **Daily Microfoliant**.
- Try décolletage patches overnight such as those made by **SK-II** and **Société**.

BEAUTY KNOW- HOW

FOUNDING PRINCIPLES

As with most things, getting the basics right is essential to mastering a great makeup routine. The key is to look like yourself, only better. Perfecting your foundation base to create flawless-looking skin is the key to a happy makeup life. It's a bit like having great hair: get this element right and everything else falls into place. Perfectly applied foundation evens out skin tone and makes it look uniform. The trick is to not over-apply, as you want your skin to look like skin, not makeup.

Finding your perfect base can be a minefield, so tracking down a friendly and knowledgeable expert is task number one. Always keep a compact mirror at the ready so you can take your colour match out into the light of day to see how it really looks, as internal lighting can play all sorts of tricks with colour. If you are navigating a colour match by yourself, you will need to test colour on your face and not the back of your hand, as your face is where the foundation is going. Experiment with three colours that you think might be your match. Place them in strips along your jawline, then take your compact mirror outside into the daylight and identify which of the colours is the hardest to see. This is your best colour match. Skin is generally paler in winter and more highly coloured in summer, so these are great times for a foundation update. Out with the old and in with the newer.

Back when the Prescriptives brand launched in Australia, all the beauty editors had individual foundation and powder shades customised, mixed and kept on file. We sat with a consultant while they played with a dazzling array of shades to come up with a perfect individualised match. Now that's service. As a general rule, yellow-based foundations are the most flattering, as they cancel out redness in the skin.

A GUIDE TO FOUNDATION

- **PRIMER** First thing's first. The first step to flawless coverage is primer; it is foundation's little helper. It improves longevity and helps prevent any patchiness. Try **Laura Mercier Foundation Primer Radiance**, which can also be worn just on its own. Primers are like an undercoat and there are multiple options to address all types of skin. **Estée Lauder** and **Dior** have great options. The latest newcomer to this category is blur cream, which shifts things up a notch, helping to disguise wrinkles and pores by using ingredients that cleverly reflect light and blur the skin. Both **Lancôme** and **L'Oréal Paris** have great versions. For both primers and blur creams, use the back of your hand as a palette and then smooth over your entire face with your fingers.

- **BB (BLEMISH BALM) CREAM** This little gem has been around for decades in Asian markets and its claim to fame is that it's a one-shot with multiple functions. It works as a moisturiser, sheer foundation, sunblock and concealer. This sounds a little like a tinted moisturiser to me, but what the heck. Try **Garnier BB Cream**. I remember when Garnier launched this category into Australia. They organised a an event with all the beauty editors in the style of *The Great Race*. Our team was called the Navy Seals and was made up of Eugenie Kelly from *Harper's Bazaar*, Sara Mclean from *Dolly* and me from *Madison*. We were pitted against our colleagues and let me tell you, it got extremely competitive. We started at the Art Gallery of New South Wales and each team had a dedicated driver. We then raced from there to Wolgan Valley in the Blue Mountains, completing all sorts of outlandish hurdles on the way, including eating as many apricots

BEAUTY KNOW-HOW

as you could stuff in your mouth, fishing for treasure in a river, painting, bike riding, cooking and wine tasting. The reward at the end of the day was worth it: a plush dinner and, best of all, sinking into the divine Wolgan Valley beds in our own private villas. Luxe.

- **CC (COLOUR CORRECTING) CREAM** It's all about the alphabet in this category. CCs stands for colour correcting and is another multi-tasking product like its sister BB cream. It is a moisturiser with a tint and sunscreen, and it also helps to disguise pigmentation. **Clinique** and **Darphin** have clever versions.

- **TINTED MOISTURISERS** Loved by all, these give a glowy light base and are what I call a 'weekend warrior', for those with flawless skin who want a tiny bit of coverage, or as a light option for weekend wear. Choose ones with an SPF coverage, moisturise and then use them as a light base. Try **La Roche-Posay 50+ Anthelios XL Tinted Cream**, or **Eve Lom** and **Hour Glass** (these two have coverage that is one step down from a liquid foundation, which I personally love).

- **LIQUID FOUNDATION** This will give you good coverage and is great as an introduction to daytime foundation. **Giorgio Armani Liquid Silk** is the gold standard in this category. Makeup artists I talk to have widely varying opinions when it comes to application tips. I prefer a blending sponge, but it can be greedy with product. Brushes are good too, but I find that I then need to blend them with my fingers to even out the coverage. Many makeup artists swear by using your fingers, as your body heat warms the foundation and makes it pliable. For starters, apply some to the back of your hand and then use your favourite applicator. Always start at the centre of your face and work out towards your hairline. Give your ears a light coat too, for uniformity.

- **CREAM FOUNDATIONS** These are the big guns, best suited to the over-30s as they can either give medium coverage or create flawless full coverage. Cream foundation comes in three consistencies: as a cream in a pot (I love **Chantecaille**), a compact like **Shiseido** or **Chanel**, or a stick – my favourite is from **Tom Ford**. It creates a lustrous finish, gives great coverage and has serious beauty bling. Stripe it on like war paint and then blend.

- **MINERAL POWDER FOUNDATIONS** I have become a devotee of this category and often use the **Piori** mineral foundation with a brush as a finishing powder over my foundation. The key to getting the coverage right is to blend, blend, blend, in circular motions with a dedicated brush over well-moisturised skin. I became a convert once I had mastered this technique. Try **Jane Iredale** and **bareMinerals**.

MAKEUP RULES
(that are meant to be adhered to and then broken)

MAKEUP IN YOUR TWENTIES

THE PALETTE This is the best your skin texture will ever be, so make the most of the tautness and luminosity. When you have a clear complexion, you can afford to skip foundation and powder and just apply a bit of concealer on any trouble spots like redness around your nose, blemishes, and under the eyes if you have dark circles. If you want to even out skin tone, try a tinted moisturiser with an SPF of at least 50. And to control shine, keep some blotting papers handy in your bag to blot the oily T-zone. The trick is to have your skin looking dewy and radiant without it dissolving into an oil slick.

ARSENAL

- Experimenting with bright lipstick in your 20s is a rite of passage, as you can get away with pretty much any lip colour, from outrageous neon pink lips – try **Nars Audacious Lipstick** in Greta – to the mattest of matte lips in anything from dark chocolate to navy blue – **Too Faced Melted Matte Long Wear Lipstick** has every shade conceivable.
- At the opposite end of the spectrum you can get away with practically no lip coverage at all. Try **Lanolips Tinted Lip Balm SPF30** in Perfect Nude for the perfect nudey gloss. Keep it carside for any eventuality.
- Blue mascara is the perfect way to play with colour around your eyes; try **Benefit Blue Mascara**. Wear it as a topcoat over your favourite black mascaraed lashes or on its own, blurred up with a blue liner along the lashline. Keep lips nude.
- Winged liner with the perfect flick. Use a business card and hold it with one end against the bridge of your nose and the other end at an angle against the outside corner of your eyelid. Then trace a line toward your

temple with liquid eyeliner like **Lancôme Artliner** and repeat on the
other side. Keep a cotton bud and eye makeup remover close at hand
just to neaten up any smudges.

- For the perfect portable foundation to touch up on the go try
  Maybelline Fit Me Shine-Free + Balance Foundation.
- At this age you can get away with blue murder as far as eye shimmer
  goes. So go for broke with **Make Up For Ever Diamond Powder** in
  Rose Gold. Wear it over the entire lid, applied with a generous brush.
- **Nars Illuminator** in Super Orgasm is worth having in your arsenal for
  the name alone. It is the perfect highlighter for just-blushed cheeks.

MAKEUP IN YOUR THIRTIES

This is the time to create a makeup capsule and splurge on the basics, such as an
illuminating primer and great foundation that evens out any flaws and has some
anti-ageing benefits to boot. Cream or powder eyeshadows in taupe, brown
and ivory are fail-safe options; I have a trio in a compact that travels with me
everywhere. When I was in my 30s I interviewed makeup guru Bobbi Brown
and she impressed on me the transforming power of blush. It wakes up your
complexion and gives you a healthy glow that you never realised you were
missing until it's pointed out. I've taken blush that one step further and often
use it as eyeshadow, swiped over my entire lid and up to my brows. There are
so many supremely wearable blush shades from peachy pink to bronzy brown.

Wake up the inner rim of your eye with a concealer-coloured eye pencil like
Shiseido or Mecca Beauty Sleep Artistry Eye Brightener, which is a fabulous
double-ended stick (one end is thick, the other thin) for highlighting and lining
that has become my travel staple. The beauty of a warmer hue is that it is closer

*BEAUTY
KNOW-
HOW*

to the natural colour of the inner rim of your eye, as opposed to the starkness of a white eyeliner. To ramp up eye definition, switch to black liner on the inner and upper rims of your eyes. The uppers take some practice, as it's a much more sensitive spot, but persistence is well worth the effort

My 30s was also the time I became my own lipstick formulator: I was always layering three or four nudes to get the perfect customised blend.

ARSENAL

- **YSL Touche Éclat**, a legendary illuminating and highlighting concealer, is a must.
- A great foundation is an essential ingredient; try **Giorgio Armani Luminous Silk Foundation**. I discovered this early on and it is still a favourite.
- Tom Ford does a great **Complexion Enhancing Primer** that I can't live without.
- For eyes, a palette is a truly great companion. I love **Urban Decay Naked** – every one of the 12 shades is a winner.
- **Lancôme Hypnose** mascara is a constant companion.
- The essential blush component has so many astonishing options. Try **Nars Blush** in Orgasm in cream or powder, **M.A.C Prabal Gurung** and anything **By Terry** just for starters.
- Get your brush kit up to speed. Essential tools include a foundation brush for wet and dry foundation and powder, eyeshadow brush, lip brush, blush brush and bronzing brush. Once you start with these the list can be endless. Start out with a travel set to see what you use the most. **Issada** do a good one.

MAKEUP IN YOUR FORTIES

Keep hold of the delightful bone and beige eyeshadow shades that were the staples of your 30s, but update with some warmer and richer tones like chestnuts, bronzes and golds. Avoid shimmer at all costs. Keep up the love affair with your eye pencil and get practised at smudging it as close to the lashes as possible. Don't neglect your brows; remember, they are the frame for your face and now is the time to embrace seeing a brow expert every six weeks to keep them looking groomed. The finishing touch is always lashings of plumping mascara; apply at least two coats.

On lips, go for peach or rosy shades, as dark colours may emphasise thinning lips and feather lines (but if you use lip fillers you won't have this problem, so bring on the colour). A little dab of gloss in the centre of the lip is a trick to keep them looking fresh. To test lip colour, give it one swipe on the ball of your index finger, as this will give you a good indication of how the colour will look on your lips. Blush is also absolutely essential; apply it high on your cheek bones to give your face a lift.

ARSENAL

- Go for a lipstick in an easy-to-wear shade. Try **Clarins Instant Light Lip Balm Perfector**.
- **Bobbi Brown Gold Eye Shadow** is easy to apply and soft on the eye.
- **Laura Mercier Stick Eye Colour** is a long-wearing cream stick shadow that can be worn as a smudgy eyeliner or full-blown eyeshadow.
- **Lancôme**, **Maybelline** and **L'Oréal Paris** mascara are all stalwarts.
- Find a creamy anti-ageing foundation that has lifting properties, such as **Diorskin Skin Sculpt**.

BEAUTY KNOW-HOW

FIFTY-PLUS MAKEUP

When it comes to makeup, the old adage 'less is more' applies. Start with updating your foundation with a creamy, dewy one, as it needs to be flexible so that it doesn't pool in facial lines. If you want to use powders, ensure they are translucent. Laura Mercier has a good array, and Priori makes great mineral powder foundations, but don't forget to blend, blend, blend, in circular motions at all costs, as you don't want to emphasise any lines.

Foundation coverage should be full-face. Choose one that is moisturising, like Lancôme Absolue Sublime Rejuvenating Essence Foundation, and always apply with a sponge like the failsafe Beauty Blender. You will use less foundation and create even coverage all over. Apply a small amount to the back of your hand and dab the blender into it, then start from the centre of your face with a stippling motion and work out.

ARSENAL

- I love making my eyes look bigger with a soft black khol pencil on the inner and upper rim of my eyes. Try **Laura Mercier Longwear Crème Eye Pencil**. On lids, try a neutral shadow to hide any redness and veins. A handy eye palette works best, one that has a great neutral shade as well as darker shades to build intensity. Try **Bobbi Brown On Trend: Eyes Sultry Bronze**.
- Defined brows are essential and a quick and easy pick-me-up is a tinted brow gel that will add a colour boost and sweep them into shape. Try **Nudestix Eyebrow Stylus Pencil and Gel**.
- Who doesn't want fuller fatter lashes? Try **Charlotte Tilbury Full Fat Lashes 5 Star Mascara**.

- A lightweight matte lipstick is the answer to all your prayers. Avoid shades with blue undertones as they can make lips appear thinner. An all-time favourite is **Chanel Rouge Allure Velvet** with flattering mother-of-pearl particles to make lips look supple.

LIP SERVICE

Because of my penchant for every conceivable shade of nude lipstick,
I love finding the perfect match for my friends as well. For me it's all about
the beauty bling too. Love, love, love Tom Ford Lip Colour in Pink Dusk,
Charlotte Tilbury lipstick in Bitch and M.A.C lipstick in Twig, for starters.
Their packaging is so divine, making up in public with these bad boys is
a must. I often customise my own nudes with a vast array of chubby sticks,
lip pencils, lipsticks, glosses and glimmer sticks. The variety is endless; often
I am asked what lipstick am I wearing, and more often that not it's some weird
and wonderful combination that I have concocted in the morning from my
vast array of nudies.

Here are some of my favourite combinations: Nudestix do some great double-
header nude Lip and Cheek Pencils. My favourite is Mystic and Whisper; I have
used it down to the nub as a base for a nude lipstick or just on its own. This range
is sheer genius. Bobbi Brown also does a fabulous Rose Brown Art Stick that
gives a knockout chocolaty base to any lipstick. For a gorgeous highlighter,
try Tom Ford Lip Shimmer in Solar Gold; placed in the centre of the lips, it adds
a super-pretty highlight to any lipstick shade. Laura Mercier Praline Cream is
another go-to favourite, while Revlon Colorburst Matte Balm in 230 provides the
perfect creamy chamois base worn on its own or as the perfect painterly undercoat
for any lipstick alive. Chanel Rouge Coco Shine Hydrating Sheer Lipshine in Boy
is fabulous for fair skin. Burberry Beauty Lip Cover in Nude Rose is a delicious
little peachy hue that works back perfectly with a bronzy palette.

I could rabbit on for days; the range of possibilities is endless. I suggest you
go out and experiment with as many nudes as possible; scratch the surface
and you will find nude-inspired lip gems everywhere.

Of course, there are other colours in the lipstick spectrum and when I was interviewing master makeup artist Dick Page in New York for the launch of Shiseido's Perfect Rouge range, the way he enthused about his love of lipstick was infectious. Dick works his magic on Julianne Moore, Isabella Rossellini, Catherine Zeta-Jones, Iman, Hope Davis and Raquel Zimmermann. His approach is 'guerilla style': he puts lipstick on with an eyeshadow brush and often uses a lip pencil afterwards, rather than before. He doesn't like anything that is too uniform, and with hard-core reds, he blends the colour into the lip a little bit, causing it to blur, or he uses a cotton bud just to diffuse the edges. My favourites from that range were Dragon Red and Mystery.

I loved his take on red lipstick. He says, 'I regard red as almost a neutral, as it is so iconic. Good red lip gloss is important but it doesn't rate as highly on the sex meter as lipstick. I am always really impressed by women who can put their lips on without looking in a mirror. Gwen Stefani can do this; I was out to dinner with her in Paris and she applied those red lips with the perfect simple gesture.'

When I am out to lunch with the beauty posse, who have all just applied their favourite mood-enhancing lipstick, invariably someone will have lipstick on their teeth. I am always at pains to alert them with that unmistakeable finger to tooth action. My friend and colleague Sherine is also obsessed with never having food caught in her teeth. She is always baring them at me after a meal to get the all-clear, and keeps a compact mirror with her at all times. The same applies to eyelashes and stray makeup-brush hairs on faces. Tell people immediately, otherwise it can get awkward. It's in the same category as the undone fly.

MAKING UP IN PUBLIC

I have my mini makeup kit on hand at all times, a smart little monogrammed Mon Purse pouch that I was given – love it. It houses my quick and easy go-to tools, including my Shiseido Natural Liquid Compact in Natural Light Ivory foundation, a genius product that I have been wedded to for 30 years. What the Japanese don't know about makeup is not worth knowing. The compact has a great mirror that folds out flat when you open it out for easy up-close application. I use Shiseido concealer pencil for the inner rim of my eyes in the most flattering putty shade, rather than a harsh white, to lighten up my eyes. At the other end of the spectrum is my Laura Mercier Eyeliner in Noir Supreme that adds an instant glam update. My M.A.C Pro Longwear Paint Pot eyeshadow in Stormy Pink is super easy to apply and doubles as a cheek blush, and Nars lip gloss in Chelsea Girls is the perfect nude gloss. My Love Those Lashes lash extension brush keeps my essential lash extensions running in the same direction, while Diorshow Brow Styler Gel keeps my brows looking groomed.

This means I am never without my war paint. I make up in the car while waiting at the lights, carefully, at my desk, in waiting rooms, on flights, on trains (okay, so I haven't been on a train in a very long time but if I were I would invariably be topping up my makeup). There are very few more therapeutic ways to spend a moment. A little slice of time out and the end result is a fresh face. There are a few grooming no-noes in public though: no hair brushing (as tempting as it might be), nail filing, tweezing, nail clipping (gross), or nail polish application.

No-mirror makeup is the bomb. My favourite lipstick in this category is Clinique Absolute lipstick in Black Honey. You can put it on with your eyes closed absolutely anywhere. It is genius and the most flattering berry tint you will ever find. The trick with mobile makeup application is to use standalone

products that don't require brushes or applicators. My weapons of choice: pencils, multi-purpose chubby sticks and cream shadows.

MAKEUP IN A FLASH

- Dab some concealer such as **Laura Mercier Secret Camouflage** on the trouble spots – blemishes, under the eyes and around the nose – then blend with the all-important gentle ring finger.

- Whip out a liquid foundation compact that comes with a sponge and lightly work over your entire face.

- Use your ring finger to apply a cream eyeshadow in universally flattering shades of brown, taupe or cream. Bobbi Brown has a fabulous **Long-Wear Cream Shadow Stick** in New Goldstone. Work the colour across your lids, taking it just up past the eye crease.

- With a cheek and lip chubby stick like **Clinique**'s, place three dots of colour on your cheeks and then blend, blend, blend in circular motions, using your middle finger.

- If you are after more definition, use a soft black kohl pencil to line the inner and upper rim of the eye. This will give great depth and make your lashes appear thicker. Try **L'Oréal Paris Color Riche Kajal**.

- Apply mascara and work the brush in a zigzag motion, applying two coats for maximum impact.

- Apply a tinted brow gel like **By Terry Eyebrow Mascara** and brush brows upwards.

- Last but by no means least is lipstick. For a light stain, use your pointer finger and dab the colour on your lips, or for a pout that packs a punch, apply the stick directly to your lips, blot and then apply another coat. This will help your lipstick last.

BEAUTY KNOW-HOW

SKINCARE AND BEAUTY GURUS

In my worldwide travels and encounters with experts, I have gleaned some tips worthy of bottling as well as some scary skincare crimes. Here are some of the highlights from the best in the business.

COSMETIC SURGEON DR JEAN-LOUIS SEBAGH

CRIME FILE 'The skin crime I see most often is lumpy, permanent skin fillers, which are sadly almost irreversible.'

TIPS 'Take off your makeup before going to bed and moisturise. I used to watch my mother doing this and never understood why she took so much time over it until much later on.'

NEW YORK FACIALIST CHRISTINE CHIN

CRIME FILE 'The sun dries out your skin and causes sun damage and wrinkles. The only solution is to apply sunblock every two hours.'

TIPS 'Cleanse, tone, and use glycolic, retinol, moisturiser and sunblock. That's what everyone's skincare regime should be for nice glowy skin.'

SYDNEY DERMATOLOGIST DR NATASHA COOK

CRIME FILE 'The most common crime is picking pimples. This creates more inflammation in the skin and therefore red marks that take 6–12 months to fade, potentially creating permanent scars. Others include using mechanical scrubs on the face and over-cleansing. This strips the barrier layer of the skin down, creating more skin problems such as dermatitis and irritation, and it makes acne worse.'

TIPS 'After applying moisturiser, place a wet cloth over the top for 30 minutes to boost the hydrating capacity. I picked up this tip when I worked in the Children's Hospital at Westmead looking after babies and young children with extremely bad eczema. Loads of moisturiser with wet wraps made the world of difference in repairing their damaged skin.'

LOS ANGELES COSMETIC DERMATOLOGIST DR KARYN GROSSMAN

CRIME FILE 'Patients should ask their practitioners for their credentials and training background.'

TIPS 'A light at-home peel: do not leave it on any longer than the instructions suggest, though.'

LONDON FACIALIST NICHOLA JOSS

CRIME FILE 'Using the wrong products. A good skin analysis and facial can always correct this.'

TIPS 'Skin loves to be massaged. It's amazing as it not only plumps skin and brings blood to the surface, but relieves tension and stress in the facial muscles. I am a big believer in internal mouth massage for firming and toning the cheek and jowls and for getting rid of tension.'

DERMATOLOGIST DR HOWARD MURAD

CRIME FILE 'People tend to over-process their skin, including exfoliating it too much, picking at the skin and using products that are incorrect for their symptoms. I believe in working with a professional who can help you to

BEAUTY KNOW-HOW

understand your skincare concerns and recommend a comprehensive three-step skincare regimen that is right for you. Your regimen should always include a gentle cleanser, a treatment product that targets your issues and a moisturiser that is specifically formulated for your specific skin concerns.'

TIPS 'I always say that smiling is a free way to look more beautiful – a smile can make you look younger and laughing is good for your soul. I also think the antioxidant potential of the yumberry (*Myrica rubra*) will really advance certain types of skincare products. Antioxidants are so important, since they are the key to protecting our skin and our bodies from the internal and environmental stresses that lead to premature aging.'

MAKEUP ARTIST DICK PAGE

CRIME FILE 'Skin often only needs a little bit of foundation here and there. The less you do, the better it looks on most people.'

TIPS 'With blush, apply cheek colour on the pillows of your cheeks before everything else, as it changes the aspect of the rest of the face, and it also makes eyes look whiter. This is sometimes all you need. Blush is supposed to be just that – something that makes you look pretty. I like blushes in red and pink as I think they animate the face. Try bronzer with the right highlighter and a little bit of blush over the top to give a little heat in the skin. With eyeliner, it is meant to go as close to the lashes as possible, not on the lids. Draw from the outside of the eye in with small strokes not one continuous line. The aim is not to see any skin between the eyeliner and the lashes.'

MAKEUP ARTIST BOBBI BROWN

CRIME FILE 'Getting foundation to match skin perfectly. All my base products, like concealer, foundation, powder and tinted moisturisers, are yellow-based to counteract redness in the skin.'

TIPS 'Blush makes you instantly prettier. Eyebrow maintenance is essential, and I always travel with my pocket marooned-on-a-desert-island compact, with concealer, foundation, lip gloss, cream blush, day lipstick (in Shimmer and Brown) and night lipstick.'

M.A.C MAKEUP ARTIST GORDON ESPINET

CRIME FILE 'Eyebrows are an ongoing story and I think it's because the fashion industry wants to make women crazy. Tweeze them all out, then grow them back, let's bleach them now, and then next time let's make them dark. Makeup artists make people crazy sometimes.'

TIPS 'Like yourself and do unto others as you would have them do unto you – in other words, don't poke anyone in the eye with a mascara wand. Makeup needs to be about a whole lot of natural. You want the makeup to be fabulous yet achievable. Now, beauty is becoming honest and more human; it is not about the retouched look. It is all about natural-looking skin using primer and a little bit of concealer. Little details are what matter. Get rid of the Instagram filters. No more plastic, please.'

BEAUTY KNOW-HOW

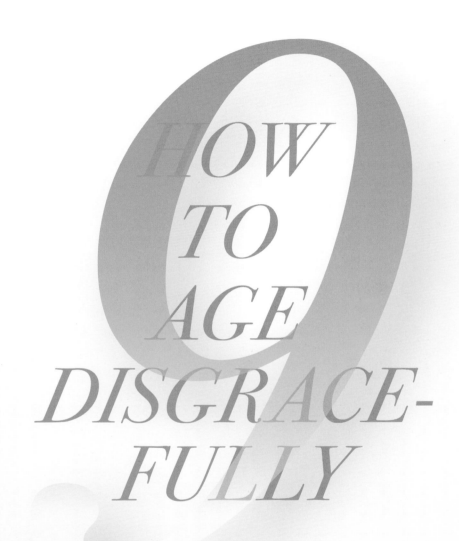

9

HOW TO AGE DISGRACE-FULLY

Y PERCEPTION OF MYSELF, AND MY CONFIDENCE, have morphed over the decades. Why couldn't I have had the confidence of my 50s in my 30s, because isn't 50 the new 30? Each decade has brought challenges and rewards. Before I became beauty director at *Sunday Life*, I was beauty director at the marvellous *Madison* magazine, where I had eight years of amazing fortune and fabulousness and worked with two great editors, Paula Joye and Lizzie Renkert, and a legendary team who made coming to work a dream. It was here that my test-driving of cosmetic procedures took off in earnest, as I put my body on the line in the pursuit of scientific excellence. Oh, okay then, in search of eternal youth.

In 2013, *Madison* was closed, and to this day I can recall second-by-second how that day unfolded. I was at a work breakfast with a gaggle of beauty editors when my editor, Lizzie Renkert, called and said I needed to come back to the office urgently as management had decided to close the magazine. The day was wet; I arrived back drenched and was then sent straight up to be offered a redundancy package along with the rest of the team. It was like a scene from *Up in the Air*: tears and numbness. The shock wave was a tsunami and the thought of not being with my beloved colleagues five days a week was inconceivable. I'm not good on my own, as you have probably guessed.

Having been under the protective mantle of full-time work for thirty years, the fear of the unknown freelance landscape was overwhelming. I am very resistant to change but this forced one has brought with it exceptional opportunities. I now work with the phenomenal Pat Ingram and the wonder team at *Sunday Life*, writing a weekly column that I adore. I go into the Fairfax office one day a week because I love the interaction and would be lost without it; and, of course, it also gives me the chance to dress up.

The thing I have also realised is that the greatest beauty asset on the planet is a smile. That may sound a bit corny but it's so true and the two people I know with the best smiles, ever, are my sons Harrison and Jonah. When those kids smile, it just takes my breath away.

In my 30-year career in magazines, the idea of ageing and how to fight it has taken up more and more of my time – funny that. I am always pushing the anti-ageing boundaries, along with every other boundary I can find, with weekly test drives for my column in *Sunday Life*. To date I have road-tested over 170 treatments (and still counting). The most painful to date was Ultherapy. The process began with an ultrasound image of my face to work out what needed attention. Those close-up, take-no-prisoner images are always confronting and require a tranquilliser before the treatment even begins.

I had my face and neck treated, and it worked like this. Radio frequencies are used to emit ultrasound waves at a depth of 4.5 millimetres to the dermal layer of your skin, surgically tightening and lifting the tissue. This ultrasound treatment bypasses the skin's surface and the energy delivered heats the collagen in your skin, which in turn stimulates the growth of fresh new collagen and elastin that then contracts and lifts the skin tissue.

So that's the factual part; now for the intensity. With a tranquilliser under my belt, I was chugging away on the happy gas, which takes the edge off, but by the end, an hour later, I was sweating bullets and was actually reduced to tears. No mean feat for me, but you know what they say, no pain no gain. My jaw was still a little sensitive even a week later. The results kick in gradually: three weeks later my jawline was definitely more defined and my face felt tauter. The outlay is not cheap at around $3500 and some might argue that putting that towards a facelift might make more sense, but I was really pleased with the results. I also have it on good authority that they have now dialled down the pain factor and the treatment is just as effective, so I'll obviously be giving that another go.

At the bliss end of the spectrum there are so many transporting treatments, but my latest favourite indulgence is the four-handed facial, which is serious sensual overload. Jocelyn Petroni (Joss to her friends) is always pushing the boundaries to create out-of-this-world facials and I was lucky enough to test-drive her latest incarnation at prototype stage. It all started with Joss deep-cleansing my face while her colleague Diandra cleansed my décolletage, shoulders and neck using a combination of European shiatsu, lymphatic drainage and reiki. The beauty of it is the four-handed pressure and massage movements that are in sync with each other and in time with my breathing. The second cleanse is vigorous and includes steam and more four-hands massage, exfoliation and extraction while your hands are massaged. A mask is then applied under warm steam as your nails are shaped and painted. It's like a five-in-one treatment.

On the test-drive front I am always up for new treatments and have a highly developed radar when it comes to practitioners and treatments; I am also lucky to have a coterie of knowledgeable advisers

who warn me off anything death defying. Over 30 years I have road-tested myriad treatments, ranging from the sublime to the ridiculous, and I rate their success by when my colleagues say I look well. Here are some edited highlights of ones that made me sigh and cry.

ONE OF MY FIRST ENCOUNTERS with more intrusive techniques was with injectable filler in my lips. I have a tendency to bruise easily and this time was no exception. I looked like Salvador Dalí complete with moustache as the bruising in my lips migrated up towards my nose. It was in the early 2000s and Australian Fashion Week was in full swing; I somehow convinced myself that no one would notice. That certainly was not the case. Since then I have had my lips topped up every couple of years, and techniques and product have improved vastly with the softer filler Juvéderm. The smooth gel fills in lip lines and wrinkles while the hyaluronic acid attracts and maintains moisture levels, which helps with the incessant chapping I suffer from. Initially there is always some swelling and a bit of a duckbill but after a couple of weeks this settles completely to create a lipstick-worthy pout.

I was also one of the first guinea pigs to trial Isolagen in Australia: a very clever concept that generates your own bank of collagen-producing fibroblasts. A small section of skin was harvested from behind my ear – this is undamaged skin because it is protected from sun exposure. These cells were then stimulated in the lab, for six weeks, to produce fibroblasts (the cells that produce collagen) and then reinjected into my wrinkles, including my nasolabial lines, as the perfectly compatible filler. The course of injections, spaced about a month apart, acted to stimulate collagen production and they claimed that results may even be permanent. That was 20 years ago and now (I have just checked in the mirror) I don't have those nasolabial lines. Of course that may be because of the 199 other treatments I have had subsequently . . . Having your own personalised filler material is a great idea and you could also have the excess material cryogenically frozen for use in the future. Sadly, Isolagen didn't go the distance here. Probably had something to do with the cost.

Sometimes the simplest treatments are the best, especially when it comes to hard-to-get-to areas like the back. I have always had a fear that my back could be harbouring some unwanted blemishes, but how do you know and how do you get to them? The answer is a back treatment with a skincare magician like Sue Dann, who uses the cult product Dr Spiller in her 'back facial'. This treatment includes cleansing, steam, exfoliation with an enzyme peel, extractions and massage with a collagen lotion, and a declogging and anti-ageing mask. End result: my back felt clean as a whistle. This is a great treatment to have prior to summer exposure.

Over the past two years I have become addicted to lash extensions, and they have revolutionised my makeup application and the way I view my face on waking up. The joy of looking in the mirror first thing and feeling more than okay is gold. Having lush, defined lashes, along with whitened teeth, rate as two of the best anti-agers I know. After a fresh set of lashes, I have even been known to apply just foundation and lip colour and that is it! When you first sign up, lash application takes roughly an hour and a half. Extensions come in all shapes, sizes, thickness and material (silk, mink and human hair) and range from 8 to 15 millimetres.

Again, finding a great practitioner is essential and I am wedded to Stella at Love Those Lashes. The latest update is 3D volume lashes, which are three silk lashes applied with a specialised glue to every one of my lashes. I toddle along every two weeks for infills, and whenever I've been away for an extended period, Stella is my first port of call when I get home.

Another find that has two-in-one appeal is Botox targeted at teeth clenching and grinding. I have been a clencher since I was 12, resulting in jaw masseter muscles that a weightlifter would be proud of. I wear a dental splint at night that protects my teeth, but I still suffer from bruxism (clenching). Dr Joseph Hkeik, who ministers my vitamin B (Botox) shots, wielded his Botox needles, injecting it into the bulk of the masseter muscles to weaken them and reduce grinding and clenching. This process relieves teeth abrasion, muscle pain and tension headaches, and as a bonus, also softens the angle of the jaw and sculpts cheekbones. After a week, the muscles relax; chewing can be a little weird initially but you soon adjust. I have had this treatment before, and at week six my jawline had softened and you could cut glass with my cheekbones. Results last six to twelve months, which reminds me I need a top-up.

*B*ELIEVE IT OR NOT, I have also tried some natural therapies that have worked wonders for me, including a facial with natural therapist Fumi Yamamoto. Fumi's treatments combine facial reflexology, acupressure point massage, facial yoga and meditation, and her mission is to get skin glowing and balanced by getting rid of toxins and delivering more nutrients to the cells through lymphatic drainage.

She works from the feet up to the head and includes a heavy-duty skull work-out. She works on the stress locked in my face, neck and those problem shoulders with muscle release techniques and essential oils, seeking out knots of stress. Ninety minutes later, my jawline and cheekbones look more defined and I seem to be standing taller. This is a great treatment for puffiness from jet lag.

*M*Y BROWS HAVE ALWAYS BEEN ON THE FAIR SIDE, so feathertouch eyebrow tattooing has been a godsend. I love having my brows shaped and dyed, as they really do frame up the face, but I am crap at maintaining them, so the fail-safe solution is brow tattooing (never fear, this is not permanent, lasting around 12 months) with brow expert Amy-Jean Linnehan. The process involves anaesthetic cream on my brows for an hour followed by Amy-Jean working her etching pen with seven sharpened tips over my brows, weaving fine, hair-like strokes between the existing hairs. There is a series of four sweeps over each brow, punctuated with application of the hypoallergenic pigment. The sensation is of sharp scratching, which is a little uncomfortable but no worse than that; a strange thing I've discovered is that my left brow is more sensitive than the right.

My brows end up looking very dark and defined, with a perfectly shaped arch. Amy tells me that they will fade by 25 to 50 per cent and settle into a very natural shade. I have to admit when I first got home and saw Harrison, he rather helpfully said I looked like a man, but fortunately, they did fade into a defined natural shade just as Amy

Jean had said they would. I needed to keep my brows dry for the first five days when showering to stop the water diluting the dye, and I also needed to keep them out of the direct sun for the first week, but this was pretty straightforward.

As I age, lifestyle takes its toll. The barely noticeable capillaries on my nose have decided to take centre stage, so addressing them is crucial. Skin clarity is the holy grail and I plan on maintaining that for as long as is humanly possible. Doctor Deborah Davies's skill at wielding the sclerotherapy needle for leg veins is legendary, so I went to see her about the capillaries on my nose. She works wonders with the yellow light delivered by the powerful Candela Vbeam Laser, combining it with 20 per cent saline solution injections. The saline injections initially weaken the veins and the yellow light from the photo-regeneration Vbeam laser then targets the red blood vessels to finish them off. I sucked on some laughing gas for a little light relief as Deborah worked her magic. The laser is a little stingy, and the injections are, as expected, quite intense, as the nose area is very sensitive. Ice is then applied to calm the area post treatment. Following the treatment I can see that most of the capillaries have gone, but there is one troublesome one still hanging in there so I am booked in for a follow-up zap. Maintenance, maintenance.

I AM ALSO ALWAYS ON THE LOOKOUT for boosting treatments, and facialist Melanie Grant is famous for weaving her facial magic with her signature treatment, #GettingReady. This can be a one-shot deal or a series of treatments to get your skin in peak condition. It entails a deep cleanse and then a diamond microdermabrasion that deeply exfoliates, polishes and buffs skin. Next step is a corrective hydrating booster and the finishing touch, the infrared Omnilux Revive light therapy. The intense infrared light works to help reduce fine lines, boost collagen and improve skin texture. The finishing touch is a moisturiser with sunscreen. If you have a big event to attend, it's best to have this one-hour treatment 24 hours prior, to give your skin time to settle.

ANOTHER BIG HIT ON THE BEAUTY RADAR was when I had my first facial threading session, and no, I am not referring to the cosmetic surgery procedure that in some cases can end up giving you cat's whiskers as the threads migrate their way to the skin's surface. Yikes. I am talking about the ancient hair removal technique that originatedin the Middle East. After cleansing, anti-bacterial organic cotton thread is worked back and forth over the face to remove any facial hair.

Post-treatment, the circulation of blood to the face is increased and this can cause redness for 24 hours and possibly a few little bumps, but my skin felt the softest and smoothest it had ever been, as the threading not only removes downy hair but also acts as an exfoliator and helps stimulate collagen production. The following day my skincare products just sank in. The next day my face looked radiant, moisturiser glided on like a dream and my foundation looked flawless.

*P*ERHAPS THE MOST UNIQUE AND INTRIGUING TREATMENT I have tried is equine therapy at Gwinganna Lifestyle Retreat in the hinterland of the Gold Coast. When I visited, I was given the heads-up by a number of the brethren that this was the bomb. It involves a psychotherapist and four horses. On entering the paddock, you choose the horse that you feel a connection with and get up close and personal with them, downloading your innermost feelings. I dissolved into tears the moment I entered the paddock, and my initial choice of horse was a disaster: he actually tried to bite me. Rejection — even more to worry about. The therapist then moved me on to my perfect match — an endearing horse called Jack, who I latched on to, sobbing into his neck. The outpouring of emotion was really overwhelming and at the end of the session I felt completely drained, yet oddly euphoric.

It is best to do this treatment midway through your stay so you can readjust and spoil yourself with luxuriating spa treatments to rebalance. What stuck with me from this session was the reminder that you can get this enduring love from your own loyal pets.

*T*HE LATEST TREATMENTS ON THE ANTI-AGEING FRONT are all about subtle improvements with tweaks here and there. Botox and filler techniques have gotten smarter and more refined, with the aim of looking fresher and healthier, rather than trying to cheat your age. The skill of the practitioner is the key to a happy outcome where you look great for your age.

The overtly Botoxed face is out, replaced by lines that are softened rather than excised; in effect a 'sprinkling' of Botox rather than a full syringe. The trout pout is over too, with the emphasis now on barely filled lips. Some 'tweakments' to try include:

FACIAL TWEAKING: Small amounts of filler, such as Restylane, are injected into the skin, to address shadowing on the face. Faces can be freshened by reducing shadowing under and above the eyes, at the temples, forehead, chin and around the nose.

TOP GUN: The latest mesotherapy incarnation comes in the form of a nine-needle hydro facial 'gun' that delivers hyaluronic acid into the dermis to give the complexion a pick-me-up in just 20 minutes. The hyaluronic acid boosts collagen and, in the process, improves skin elasticity and banishes dullness.

CHIN UP: Chiselling Chin liposculpture is strategically targeted at the ageing, sagging neck. A blunt cannula is worked over the area through tiny incisions, targeting excess fat deposits with a fluid that contains local anaesthetic and adrenalin. Post procedure, the chin is more defined and results continue to improve over the next six months.

LIP SERVICE: Lip treatments have come a long way and the latest quick fix for deflated lips is artfully placed dermal filler for plumper, more hydrated lips. The filler is injected into the lip pads and at the corner of the mouth to address loss of collagen, elastin and hyaluronic acid.

SKINCARE THAT WORKS

- Hyaluronic acid holds more that a thousand times its own weight in water and plumps the skin.
- Retinol is a derivative of vitamin A, great for targeting fine lines and wrinkles as well as sun damage. Must be used in conjunction with a high SPF as it makes skin more susceptible to sun damage.
- AHAs and BHAs dissolve dead skin cells and are good for clogged pores. Note: don't overuse them, once or twice a week is ideal.
- Sunscreen with an SPF50+: sun damage is the greatest skin ager in the business. UVA (causes ageing) and UVB (burning and skin cancer) rays damage the collagen and elastin fibres that underpin the skin.
- Antioxidants fight free radicals on the skin, so choose a moisturising formula that has them added.
- Vitamin C: take a supplement orally and apply it topically to help with sun damage and luminosity.

Australians spend a whopping one billion dollars on cosmetic surgery procedures and treatments annually and this has a lot to do with the high level of sun damage we incur, resulting in premature ageing of the skin. Time for a reminder of the golden rule of skincare: wear an SPF50+ every day, please. Rather alarmingly, according to plastic surgeon Warwick Nettle, 'People's attractiveness is rather hastily judged in the first 15 seconds and – surprise, surprise – women are the harshest judges.'

ARM LIFT (BRACHIOPLASTY)

Beyond a shadow of a doubt Michelle Obama has the best arms in the business. For those of us less fortunate, an arm lift is an extreme option. This procedure removes the excessive batwing skin and fat that can plague the upper arm. The surgery entails making an incision from the elbow to the armpit and is performed in hospital under general anaesthetic. Excess fat is first removed by liposuction, and then excess skin is pared back. As with all body contouring surgery, a scar is the trade-off for an improved contour. Maybe consider some push-ups and weight training before opting for this.

BOTOX

This is pretty much the gold standard in the fight against time with its vast array of clever cosmetic uses: wrinkle relaxing, mini brow lift, Nefertiti lift (the jowls are tightened using strategically placed Botox injections causing the neck and jowl area to lift), enhancing the Cupid's bow . . . It's all in the delivery: when it is artful it freshens the face; when it's not, the face can end up looking frozen. Botox lasts between four and six months. It is so addictive that you need to resist the urge to over-inject – as with so many things in life, less is more. The latest spot for delivery is in the platysmal bands, aka the

HOW TO AGE
DISGRACEFULLY

lines around the neck. This treatment is also great for relieving excessive sweating and can help in the treatment of migraines.

In my beauty rulebook, there are two standouts: never, ever cut your own hair or inject your own Botox. Can you believe that anyone would do either of those things? People, Botox should always be administered by a professional, but I hear that this doesn't always happen. I don't know about you, but anyone who comes anywhere near me with a needle, and particularly my face, needs pristine credentials: a doctor with at least an MBBS or a registered nurse working under the supervision of a doctor.

BOOB JOB

The boob job has now been around for 50 years, and there have been times when its course has been a little rocky. There was an issue with PIP implants where industrial-grade silicone was used rather than the more expensive medical-grade silicone. This made them more prone to rupture. As a result, some of the medical bodies in Australia are now calling for a breast implant registry in Australia to track the use of implants; this is still being negotiated.

The innovative 'furry Brazilians' (P-ure or polyurethane-coated implants), on the other hand, are going from strength to strength. They have a furry outer shell (as opposed to the traditional smooth outer shell), which helps decrease the possibility of capsular contracture. This can occur when the collagen fibres in the surrounding breast tissue tightens and squeezes the implants. Because the Brazilian implants are furry, they adhere to the breast tissue and counteract the breast implant problems of sagging, thanks to their unique Velcro effect, and hardening, as a result of their lattice-like structure.

The surgery usually takes one to two hours. Cohesive silicone gel implants are the latest innovation as they feel more natural. There are many factors to be discussed with the surgeon, such as whether to place the implant underneath or on top of the muscle. Incisions are made in the crease under the breast, around the nipple areola, or in the armpit.

COLLAGEN REMODELLING

As we age, the collagen in the skin breaks down, resulting in sagging and wrinkles. One procedure that's been developed to target this is Thermage, which delivers non-invasive skin tightening and contouring in a single treatment utilising radiofrequency energy. It is great for fixing a lack of definition around the jawline, hooding on the upper eyelids, wrinkles and fine lines around the eyes, and even love handles.

Pfizer is testing an experimental anti-ageing wonder drug called Capromorelin. This new drug stimulates the body to produce the growth hormone the way it did during adolescence. During the teen years, the body increases the production of growth hormones, which are associated with building lean muscle mass and lipolysis (the breakdown of fat cells). As we age, growth hormone levels gradually decrease, causing a loss of muscle and an increase in fat. Capromorelin may help increase the levels of growth hormone; however, this is still a long way off.

DERMAROLLER

This is a medical device that 'fertilises your face'. The Dermaroller is a cylindrical drum made up of 192 micro needles which finely penetrate the skin to help deliver skincare ingredients deeper into the dermis.

It is two-pronged as it also helps stimulate and improve microcirculation. This is a great treatment if you suffer from a dull complexion, open pores, wrinkles or scarring. First, skin is numbed with an anaesthetic cream for an hour, which takes the edge off any pain factor, and then the skin is ready for the treatment. Post treatment, skin can be quite flushed and red but this settles pretty much by the following day. Three treatments are recommended, six to eight weeks apart.

EYELASH TRANSPLANTS

For me it's all about eyelash extensions, which I am highly addicted to. But this procedure takes it one big step further. Under a local anaesthetic, hair follicles are removed from the back of the scalp, individually placed into a series of incisions made in the top and bottom eyelids and then sewn into place. Queasy yet? Precision placement is essential to ensure the implanted hair will grow in the same way as existing lashes. Eyebrow transplants are also done in a similar way. Because they come from head hair, they need to be trimmed monthly and curled daily because they obviously behave like head hairs.

FRAXEL DUAL

This process treats pigmentation, sun damage, open pores and other surface skin imperfections. (It is sometimes used in conjunction with Thermage as a double whammy to incorporate skin tightening too.) Fraxel uses microscopic laser columns that penetrate deep into the skin to stimulate the production of collagen and elastin. It improves texture and skin tone and helps reduce fine lines and wrinkles. As topical local anaesthetic is applied, there is virtually no pain, but at the end of the treatment there is a fair amount of redness and some swelling. The first time I had it done, of course I convinced myself that I looked fine, in spite of the fact that my face was so swollen I could barely see out of the slits I had for eyes. Needless to say things have improved. Be prepared to peel quite dramatically, but the revelation of the new skin makes it all worthwhile.

GADGET

The Beauty Mouse helps target cellulite at home with 480 micro needles that help deliver cellulite treatment cream deeper into the skin. It also helps with microcirculation and works with any cellulite cream; try Dermaquest Dermafirm.

HAIR REMOVAL

The Candela laser takes approximately five minutes to treat bikini line and underarms and about 15 to 25 minutes to treat larger areas such as the legs or arms. Eight to ten treatments are usually the go, spaced roughly six weeks apart to tie in with the hair's growth cycle. Fake tanning and waxing are banned during the treatment phase. I would rate this treatment as one of my all-time must-haves. I recently had an all-over body treatment just to target any strays that might have crept to the surface again.

INJECTABLE FILLERS

New fillers are constantly appearing on the horizon in the battle to smooth out facial folds and wrinkles and volumise lips and cheeks. Juvéderm and Restylane are good for the face, neck, décolletage, lips and the backs of the hands.

Juvéderm is a cross-linked hyaluronic-acid-based clear gel, which is injected into the lips with an ultra-fine needle to create fuller lips. No skin test is needed, there is no downtime and results are immediate. There will be some initial swelling and sometimes bruising for a couple of days. Results last from three to eight months.

JOWLS

Juvéderm with Lidocaine is a dermal filler with local anaesthetic, so there's less pain. The results last up to 12 months and it is great for treating troublesome jowls and marionette lines. This hyaluronic acid filler can contour and volumise cheeks and the jawline to create a younger-looking profile. The next rung up is neck and chin liposuction which I have test-driven with Dr Meaghan Heckenberg. By the six-month mark the results are quite phenomenal. There is quite a lot of bruising but the spring-back results are really good and it means avoiding (or postponing) going under the knife.

KNIFE

The S-Lift (named for an S-shaped incision that is made in front of the ear) is a facelift that gives a boost to the neck and lower two thirds of the face. The skin is lifted and the surgeon tightens and re-positions the muscles and tissue and removes excess fat. The procedure takes around two hours and there will be bruising and swelling for around three weeks, but you can return to work at around day four. Also on the radar is the deep plane facelift, which works to tighten and re-anchor underlying facial tissues, producing a more natural look and longer-lasting result. It involves limited dissection under the skin, preserving the lymphatics and minimising swelling. The surgeon then dissects below the SMAS (superficial musculoaponeurotic system) layer, releasing it completely from the underlying muscles. The mid-face fat is then freed completely by dividing the cheek ligaments, which tether it to the cheekbones beneath. Once this is done, the whole face can be lifted vertically. The now-mobile SMAS layer can then be re-anchored higher up the face. This lift creates a long-lasting improvement to the jawline, neckline and cheekbones and there is no pulled appearance, since the whole face is evenly lifted. As you can imagine, it ain't cheap.

LIQUID LIPO

This is a fat-blasting technique that is much less traumatic than the original liposuction procedures. It uses a fine jet of high-pressure water applied with a cannula to separate and break down fat cells without damaging surrounding tissue. Only mild sedation is required, which means that you can stand up during the procedure for any tweaking that is required. You need to wear a pressure garment and stay in bed for a day, and the leaking of excess fluid from the incisions is a little weird, but you can do light activities for the following two days and go back to your normal routine after that. Results are immediate and continue to improve over the next six weeks.

MACROLANE

This is the boob jab that we are still waiting for. It is a thickened form of hyaluronic acid that can be used as a soft tissue enhancement filler for slight breast enlargement and filling out flat bottoms. It is applied with a healthy dose of local anaesthetic. It lasts from one to two years and is then reabsorbed by the body, but it is still awaiting TGA approval.

NECK MUSCLE IN LIPS

In the ongoing search for longer-lasting results, surgeons are becoming more and more inventive. How's this for novel? A doctor in the US, Dr Anurag Agarwal, is using a technique that grafts neck muscle on to the face to enhance lips. Surgery is simple and after the swelling goes down (usually in two weeks) you can expect results to last two years.

OTOPLASTY

This is surgery to change the appearance of a person's ears, including ear pinning, size reduction or reshaping. An incision is made at the back of the ear using a laser, and skin is then removed to expose the ear cartilage, which is then folded on itself to reshape the ear with sutures. The operation can take up to five hours depending on the problem, but as a laser is used there is minimal bruising and swelling.

PERT BOTTOM LIFT

The butt lift was originally devised by Brazilian-born Dr Ivo Pitanguy and is now more commonly known as gluteoplasty. The procedure lifts and tightens the skin of the buttocks and may involve the insertion of silicone implants. After surgery there is pain and discomfort and you need to wear a special bandage for two to three weeks. Allow three months for the swelling to resolve and the buttocks to settle into their final appearance. In Australia there are a few different variations on the surgery available. Dr Laith Barnouti gets requests for the Pippa, the J-Lo or the Kim Kardashian butt. Buttock augmentation is done with Brazilian implants (made out of highly cohesive silicone). This involves a single 7 centimetre incision, and the buttock muscle is then divided to create a pocket for the implant. The second technique involves fat transfer, a procedure that involves harvesting fat from the same patient, purifying it and re-injecting it into the buttock area. This is a minimally invasive procedure where 50 per cent of the injected fat will dissolve in the first six weeks and the remainder will remain.

SUBQ

Restylane SubQ is great for sculpted cheekbones, but beware the 'pillow face' syndrome that makes a face look over-filled. Again, skilful administration is vital so a light-handed practitioner is the key to a happy face. SubQ is good for correcting sagging and a drooping jawline. It is thicker than traditional Restylane and is injected under the muscle. The process takes about 30 minutes and then three to four days for the swelling to settle down.

RESURFACING

Diamond Head Microdermabrasion is a super-duper form of exfoliation that removes gluey dead surface skin cells and stimulates new ones to grow. In practical terms, this means fresher, healthier-looking skin. The exfoliation process occurs when a diamond-tipped head makes contact with the skin and abrades it; the dead skin cells are then suctioned away. This is great for solving congestion and giving a boost to dull skin.

STEM CELLS

Adult stem cells are the great white filler hope and are revolutionising cosmetic procedures just as lasers once did. When the technique is perfected, it will be a great two-in-one procedure as fat can be removed from unwanted areas of the body, the stem cells are then extracted and processed, mixed back with some of the fat, and then injected back into the face to fill wrinkles, lift and contour.

The beauty of this technique is that these cells are perfectly programmed to your unique genetic makeup and take about three months to integrate into your system, becoming permanent, as they are not broken down by your body. This is the way of the future.

Cytori is one to watch for too. This treatment was developed to reconstruct breasts after a mastectomy. Fat cells are extracted with liposuction from areas rich in fatty tissue like the tummy, buttocks and thighs. American company Cytori has recently developed a device that separates stem cells from fat and prepares them for reinjection to assist the tissue to regenerate. David Oxley of Cytori is 'thrilled that we finally have the potential to improve patients' lives using their own regenerative cells'. The fat is placed into a Celution device and processed using a mix of enzymes that digest the fat tissue, thus freeing the stem cells. The stem cells are then combined with some of the remaining fat cells, making a mixture of the stem and regenerative cells. The whole process takes about two hours. This power-packed solution provides volume and can fill up the 'divot' made by a lumpectomy and the empty 'skin pouch' of a mastectomy. Doctors inject the fat and stem cell solution, droplet by droplet, into the treatment area after making tiny cuts that penetrate the scar tissue and turn it into a 'biological mesh'. Breasts that have been damaged by breast cancer treatment are good candidates for this treatment. On average, cup size will increase by one or two sizes and treatment can be repeated every three to four months, as long as there are sufficient levels of donor fat in other areas of the body. Stem cell transfer also opens up possibilities for breast, buttock and facial enhancements.

TEAR TROUGHING

This treats the hollow area that can appear under the eyes caused by loss of volume in the face. First, anaesthetic cream is applied, followed by the injection of a dermal filler like Juvéderm Ultra, which is placed just above the orbital rim and then massaged to achieve the best contour. It takes 30 minutes, and you should take it easy for the first 24 hours, avoiding rubbing your eyes.

ULTHERAPY

Ultrasonic energy heats the dermis to a depth of 4 to 7 millimetres to deliver a tightening effect, over two to three months, to the facial contours and skin using ultrasound technology. According to plastic surgeon Dr Warwick Nettle, 'Nothing will lift and firm as effectively as surgery, but Ultherapy is an in-office procedure with no downtime. I tell my patients the effects are subtle, but real.' The sensation is really intense so painkillers before the procedure are essential. Ultherapy triggers the body's natural healing response, resulting in new and improved collagen with no downtime.

VAMPIRE FACIAL

This is platelet injection therapy, in which 10 to 20 millilitres of your blood is taken and spun in a centrifuge machine to extract the platelet-rich plasma, which is thought to be high in growth factor. This is then reinjected, just like a dermal filler, into your face. The growth factors in the plasma then help stimulate the collagen. Topical anaesthetic is applied and then come the injections. This started out okay, but the needle is long and by the end of the hour I was well and truly over it, as the discomfort level was quite high. There are several hundred needle pricks, and bruising and swelling do occur. It takes five days to return to normal and over the next three to six weeks you will see results, with skin appearing plumper and smoother.

WAVELENGTH LIGHT TREATMENT

Omnilux is a non-surgical, healing infra-red light therapy that plumps skin by stimulating the skin's own moisture renewal process. This is a great photo-facial for sun-damaged and ageing skin. Just lie back and bathe in the soothing infra-red light for half an hour. A course of eight to ten treatments is recommended.

X-RATED

Labiaplasty is a surgical procedure that will reduce or reshape the inner or outer labia for comfort or aesthetic reasons. The operation takes about an hour and patients are usually able to walk comfortably within a few days and resume sex in four to six weeks. And for the true devotees, there's My New Pink Button, a temporary dye 'to restore the youthful pink colour back to your labia', which lasts 48 hours. What will they think of next?

Another in the X-rated category that I wanted to squeeze in is Xeomin: it contains the same active ingredient as Botox, botulinum toxin, without the additives (complexing proteins). It doesn't need refrigeration as it comes in a fluffy cake form and is stable at room temperature. The injector just adds preserved saline and the product is ready to inject. In theory, the purity of its composition decreases the likelihood of anyone developing a resistance to it.

YOUNGER HANDS

Don't neglect your hard-working hands, which often look older than the rest of you due to neglect and overexposure to pretty much everything. Also, as we age, bones, tendons and ligaments become more pronounced along with pigmentation and loss of texture. The two factors that make hands look aged are change of texture and pigmentation. Intense Pulse Light (IPL) is your first line of defence. The pulsed light removes dark spots on hands, improves texture and encourages the production of collagen. The dermal volumising filler Radiesse is often used in the backs of the hands to create volume and generate the formation of new collagen. It starts with local anaesthetic injections, which are quite painful but brief, to numb the hands. Then a cannula is used to administer the Radiesse in a fan-like formation. Once you leave the surgery you need to massage the hands in the same fan pattern for the next few hours to keep the filler evenly dispersed. There is some tenderness and swelling initially and hands do look plumper. When I had it done, my hands felt a little tender and swollen but were fine by the following day.

ZZZZZZZZ

Night-time rescue is a favourite category of mine; I love the idea of a product working away while I sleep. The all-rounder post-surgery recovery gel, Cosmedix Rescue balm, will help soothe skin post treatment, as well as adding a big moisture boost to parched skin.

10

THE ULTIMATE EDIT

*I*N MY LONG CAREER IN BEAUTY I HAVE TRIED AND TESTED rivers of foundation and swallowed kilos of lipstick, and I'm always on the quest to find the most effective products, past and present. Some are oldies but goodies and some are new kids on the block. All I know is that they just keep coming, thick and fast.

My beauty motto is: always be at the ready, you never know when you might run into an old boyfriend. I have always taken this mantra to the extreme, even wearing 12-centimetre heels when I was on my daily pilgrimage from the Domain car park in Hyde Park (complete with hard-to-dismount moving footway) to the Bauer Media office in Park Street. I apply the same principle to good hair days, fresh lipstick and great foundation. Makeup is a powerful thing.

As a beauty director working from home, all the thousands of products that used to come to me at my office now come to my house. My fitness levels have improved markedly as I am up and down those stairs like a jackrabbit. I never tire of the joy of opening each beauty parcel to see what is coming up next. As I said at the beginning of this book, it is my dream job and has been for over 30 years, and yes, I am still living the dream!

When I had just started out as the beauty editor at *Vogue*, I did a story on my favourite 100 beauty products at the time. It was quite controversial on some levels and made me realise the power of the press.

THE
ULTIMATE
EDIT

I wanted to revisit that here, seeing which of my favourites from that time have lasted the distance and which are new contenders.

While I was struggling with corralling my favourites, I decided to ask other beauty aficionados (former and current beauty editors and, most importantly, my friends), what their all-time can't-live-without product is. Here's what they came up with.

'YSL Touche Éclat because it can cover up a multitude of sins!'
Edwina McCann, editor-in-chief, *Vogue Australia*

'I've been using M.A.C Face and Body so long I can put it on with one hand in the car while driving on the freeway and not even look in the mirror. It's sheer and buildable and makes me look healthy when I'm not. I've been in a relationship with it longer than my husband, and when they eventually change the formula – which they've been talking about for years – I'll be that woman rocking in a corner not knowing how to go on.'
Justine Cullen, editor, *Elle Australia*

'Genaissance de La Mer The New Serum Essence is a decadent serum that transforms your skin in two weeks. It's basically a super-potent version of the miracle broth that's in all their products, which you apply twice a day, and follow with a moisturiser. The payoff is a radiant, clear, plump complexion that has you forgoing foundation in no time. The only gripe I have with it is the price – this stuff is a dangerous addiction to develop.'
Eugenie Kelly, deputy editor/beauty director/features director, *Harper's Bazaar Australia*

'M.A.C Lip Pencil in Spice – an average eight pencils are sold every day in Australia.'
Kerrie McCallum, editor-in-chief, *Delicious*,
and editorial director, *Stellar*

'My favourite product is very humble: Sorbolene cream in huge pump bottles, which I use as a cleanser for face and body to preserve the delicate balance of the skin. My late beautician, Sylvia Deitch, started me on this routine in my twenties and suddenly all my inherent skin sensitivities and reactions went away.'
Karin Upton Baker, former editor-in-chief, *Harper's Bazaar Australia*

'I love experimenting with new fragrances, but the one perfume I always go back to is Acqua di Parma Gelsomino Nobile. It's a sexy, sophisticated blend of jasmine, tuberose and orange blossom, and it reminds me of being a newlywed in New York City. Now it's the finishing touch before a date night with my husband.'
Janna Johnson O'Toole, beauty and fitness director, *Elle Australia*

'SkinCeuticals Phloretin CF Gel. This free-radical-fighting antioxidant gel protects against UVA / UVB rays, evens skin tone and encourages collagen production. It goes on every morning underneath my other non-negotiable, SPF.'
Sherine Youssef, beauty editor, *Marie Claire*

THE
ULTIMATE
EDIT

'RMS Lip Shine in Moment. Makeup artist Rose-Marie Swift picked out this terracotta lip colour for me, because the tones in it help to balance lips that can throw a little blue. It's a colour she first mixed up for Gisele for the same reason. Deceptively muddy in the pot, it's not a colour I would have ever picked up without her, but I've been enjoying its lovely nude freshness every day since.'
Amy Starr, beauty and lifestyle associate, *Elle Australia*

'Lanolips, for sheer practicality. It's the ultimate multi-use salve and it hydrates and heals beautifully. Mum always used lanolin on me as a kid, but it was the stinky stuff you buy in an unmarked jar from the chemist. Was thrilled when Kirsten Carriol [Lanolips creator] brought out a handy little tube of the stuff.'
Sigourney Cantelo, founder of Beauticate

'My all-time favourite beauty product is – *gasp!* – one that I made myself, Go-To Face Hero. I've always loved rosehip oil, but knew I could boost the antioxidant and anti-inflammatory benefits by adding a smorgasbord of additional plant and nut oils for a deeply nourishing, lightweight super bloody mega oil. I swear by it.'
Zoë Foster Blake, CEO and founder of Go-To Skin Care

'My all-time favourite beauty product is Nars All Day Luminous Weightless Foundation. Highly pigmented but the finest texture, it's perfect skin in a bottle.'
Leigh Campbell, lifestyle editor, *Huffington Post Australia*

'Getting salon-like waves and bounce was always elusive until
I discovered the Cloud Nine Wide Iron. It has too many features
to list but the ceramic plates, five temperature settings and
hibernation mode set it apart from other irons. It can transform fairly
unremarkable, air-dried hair into runway-worthy waves in minutes.
Four minutes to be exact. The wide barrel ensures it doesn't take
on those lollipop curls and if you want to straighten your hair,
the wide barrel does the job in seconds.'
Rachael Mannell, freelance beauty journalist

'I can't live without my Shu Uemura eyelash curler! If I'm in
a rush I'll forgo my whole makeup bag and just give my lashes
a little squeeze – it makes such a difference!'
Alexis Teasdale, lifestyle director, *Cosmopolitan*

'Over the past eight years, not a morning or night have gone
by where I haven't applied three or four drops of SK-II Facial
Treatment Essence. It's packed full of amino acids, organics acids,
vitamins and minerals derived from Pitera. Applied after cleansing
but before serum, it rehydrates, rejuvenates and illuminates my
skin beautifully.'
Eleanor Pendleton, editor and publisher, *Gritty Pretty Magazine*

'Mascara is my fave for sure! At the moment Diorshow.'
Kirstie Clements, author

*THE
ULTIMATE
EDIT*

'My one can't-live-without product is La Prairie Advanced Marine Biology Tonic. It tones and refreshes my skin and leaves it looking radiant.'
Shonagh Walker, beauty writer

'Bioderma Sensibio H2O looks like plain old water, but don't be fooled – this wonder cleanser is impressively effective at removing makeup and leaving skin spick and span, all without disturbing even the most delicate dermis.'
Katrina Lawrence, beauty writer

'This has to be Dermalogica Pure Light SPF50: the best facial sunscreen ever. It's lightweight, gives a great sheen to the skin and has anti-ageing ingredients. A multi-tasking genius.'
Sarah Brooks-Wilson, beauty presenter

With the boundless beauty booty I am sent every minute, I still manage to have a collection of favourites that often have a history. Take for instance my Bobbi Brown Metallic Lipstick in Pretty Pink, which Bobbi Brown gave me as my 'perfect pink' after I interviewed her in New York. I wore it until it was literally down to a stump so I rang them, only to be told that sadly it had been discontinued. WHAT!!!! I was bereft and begged her to try and see if there was one still in captivity. I had to settle for a replacement Creamy Matte Lip Colour in Think Pink, but this too has now become a favourite.

This got me thinking, so I straw polled some friends to see if they had ever lost a cosmetic lifeline in this way. This may sound dramatic but some people will go to any lengths to locate a long-lost favourite. Fashion stylist Nicole Bonython-Hines was traumatised by the loss of By Terry Lumiere Velouté. 'They're saying it's been "retired" – same diff, can't bloody get it!' The thing she loved about it was its great matte coverage but that it still looked dewy and went on evenly.

Printebebe designer Fiona Kowalski said, 'The saddest thing is no Helmut Lang scent! Perfectly powdery and the most distinct yet subtle smell. Simply beautiful. I wore it for years, then he sold the company and they stopped making it. Nothing else comes close.'

For a moment in time, Kusco Murphy Lavender Crème was lost to my son Harrison, but fortunately it made a comeback. This hair cream works wonders on his textured hair and we know how fussy boys can be! I tried to track it down everywhere and finally found the creator, who said she had, after months of looking, found new formulators for this wonder product.

THE
ULTIMATE
EDIT

THE DARLING'S TOP 100
(for now)

After much gnashing of teeth, and with the proviso that this is an ongoing work-in-progress as there are still so many beauty packages yet to be opened, here goes my pick, in no particular order. They are all my babies . . .

SKIN

- **COSMEDIX RESCUE+ INTENSE HYDRATING BALM & MASK** This is one of those calming products that can soothe any skincare emergency. It is what I slather on to soothe my skin after cosmetic surgery procedures that may have irritated it.

- **ELIZABETH ARDEN EIGHT HOUR CREAM** This has been referenced a zillion times before in cult line-ups, but that's for a reason. Elizabeth used it to minister to her beloved horses for cuts and bruises and Sir Edmund Hillary used it as he climbed Mount Everest. It also soothes lips and smooths flyaway hair, is a great highlighter for cheeks, prevents lips chapping, helps repair cuticles and polishes up your favourite shoes. Two tubes of Eight Hour Cream are sold every minute around the world.

- **CLARINS BEAUTY FLASH BALM** While we're on the subject of eternal must-haves, this one is a beauty cabinet essential. This little beauty doubles as an instant pep-up mask or primer.

- **SKINMEDICA TNS ESSENTIAL SERUM** is a hardworking serum that combines the benefits of growth factor, antioxidants and peptides. Oprah loves it and so do I.

- **ULTRACEUTICALS ULTRA UV PROTECTIVE DAILY SHIELD MINERAL DEFENCE SPF50+** You know what a Nazi I am about wearing sunscreen and this one is a great everyday defence. I love its light, easy-to-wear texture.

- **GUERLAIN ISSIMA MIDNIGHT SECRET** is an oldie but a goodie and is, just as the name suggests, great for facial hangovers or as an instant pick-me-up after a long day.

- **ACTINICA LOTION SPF50+** runs neck and neck with Ultraceuticals Daily Shield and, as I like to have sunscreens stationed at every vantage point, this one resides in my glove box for essential SPF top-ups.

- **AVEDA ESSENTIAL BACK TREATMENT** is a deep cleansing masque for the back, shoulders and neck. Now if I could just get someone to apply that for me, please?

- **SUBTLE ENERGIES MOGRA (THE OIL OF JOY) & INDIAN ROSE GOLD** is a lustrous Ayurvedic aromatherapy moisturiser that is great to take travelling.

- **ELEMIS CLEANSING BALM** Where do I start? Absolutely everything about this product makes it cult, from the soothing smell to the luxe consistency and its awesome cleansing power.

- **EVE LOM THE CLEANSER** I had so much difficulty trying to decide between the Elemis Cleansing Balm and this one that I just had to include both. Have one for home and one for travel. Legendary London facialist Eve Lom launched this hero in 1985. It combines chamomile, hops, clove, eucalyptus oil and cocoa butter and comes with a muslin cloth that is an integral part of the cleansing and exfoliating process.

- **SODASHI CALMING ROSE FACE MIST** This is my deskside companion and I spritz it on on a regular basis to revive me as I rifle through my parcels and plan my next beauty column.

- **SOCIÉTÉ REJUVENATING PEPTIDE MASK** This travels with me everywhere. The act of peeling it out of the package and placing it on my parched face is a joy.

THE
ULTIMATE
EDIT

- **COSMEDIX EYE GENIUS** This is my go-to eye product as it has actives that target puffiness, dark circles and fine lines.
- **ADVANCED NIGHT REPAIR** Also affectionately known as ANR, this product works away tirelessly while you sleep.
- **L'ORÉAL PARIS WATERPROOF EYE MAKE-UP REMOVER** It just does what it says it will, and the proof is in the pudding as this stalwart sells its socks off and is a staple in many a makeup artist's beauty arsenal.
- **SISLEY BLACK ROSE CREAM MASK** An anti-ageing mask full of potent plant-based ingredients that smooth and plump tired skin. Ten minutes is all it takes.
- **GARNIER MICELLAR CLEANSING WATER** I have always been a huge fan of cleansing waters and this one doubles as a makeup remover and cleanser in one. It's great for removing excess sebum, impurities, grime and makeup with one swipe. This is the perfect product for those of us too lazy to go through a cleansing ritual at night. Who, me?
- **SMITH'S ROSEBUD SALVE** I first discovered this little gem – which hails from Woodsboro, Maryland, USA – when I was trawling through a niche little pharmacy in uptown New York. It is a travel essential, with its soothing properties for cracked lips, nappy rash, rough cuticles and hands. It was formulated by Dr GF Smith in 1895 and includes rose oils and botanicals, housed in the distinctive, collectable airtight tin.
- **HOURGLASS LIP OIL** A joy to behold and backstage favourite. This long-lasting lip treatment, with its 24-carat gold-plated tip, combines botanicals, vitamins and essential oils to hydrate and protect, and lasts for hours.
- **SOLAR D VITAMIN D FRIENDLY SUNSCREEN** Getting adequate doses of vitamin D from the sun without risking skin cancer is a perennial problem. This Australian-made sunscreen has come up with a solution:

it screens the harmful UV rays while 'permitting the particular UVB rays through that allow your body to produce vitamin D'.

- **DERMAQUEST CLEANSING OIL** I am mad for this product. I use it as pre-cleanse before I apply my cleansing balm.
- **NUXE RÊVE DE MIEL ULTRA-NOURISHING LIP BALM** One of these is sold every minute worldwide. It is a great multi-tasker and can be used as a cuticle balm and brow tamer. It keeps dry, cracked lips (mine) hydrated during the drying winter months.

TOOLS TO LIVE BY

- **DOVE COTTON TIPS** These are a great all-rounder. They can smudge out eyeliner or neaten up a lip line, and dipped in makeup remover they can remove stubborn eye makeup residue.
- **CLARISONIC PLUS SKIN CARE FACE AND BODY BRUSH** The latest automated whiz cleansing-brushes take washing your face to new levels. I love the fact that they're shower friendly and double as an exfoliator, making skin more receptive to absorbing active skincare ingredients.
- **CHANEL LE COTON** For pure indulgence you just can't go past these gorgeous hand-picked cotton makeup remover pads.
- **SHU UEMURA EYELASH CURLER** This is, beyond a shadow of a doubt, the best eyelash curler in the world.
- **TWEEZERMAN TWEEZERS** These have serious cult credibility, having won *Allure*'s Best of Beauty for nine years in a row!
- **ISSADA MAKEUP BRUSH SET** Everyone should own a makeup brush set. It takes makeup application into a new stratosphere and gives so much more control, along with the ability to blend, blend, blend. This set has been crafted from the same aluminium that is used in aircraft landing gears.

THE ULTIMATE EDIT

- **GHD ECLIPSE PROFESSIONAL STYLER** For hot iron addicts, this is a name to conjure with. It has quick-acting sensors that heat styling plates to an optimal 185°C to close the cuticle and smooth the hair.
- **CLOUD NINE WAND** I have only recently discovered the joys of wanding my hair at home and that is due to the simplicity of this little beauty. Heats in an instant, props itself up and even I can wield it to good effect.
- **TANGLE TEEZER SALON ELITE** This detangling super brush has won loads of awards and is a hair must-have, beloved by hairdressers the world over for combing through conditioner and detangling hair, no matter how knotty. This product is sheer genius – keep it shower-ready at all times.
- **PARLUX 385 POWERLIGHT CERAMIC & IONIC DRYER IN BLUSH** I love this dryer to bits and the colour is so on trend. With its combination of 2150 watts of power in a lightweight frame, it follows in the illustrious footsteps of its forebears and is adored by professional hair stylists the world over for its drying power.
- **MASON PEARSON PURE BRISTLE & NYLON POCKET BRUSH** A mix of bristle and nylon and very handbag-friendly. This brush is not cheap but still has a cult following, selling several thousand every year here.
- **M.A.C 217 BLENDING BRUSH** This oval-shaped blending brush is worthy of the beauty hall of fame for its perfect pigment placement.

BODY BASICS

- **TOM FORD SHIMMERING BODY OIL** If the look-at-me appeal of this oil was not enough to send it into cult orbit, the stats also speak volumes. It sold out in five hours when it launched at Bergdorf Goodman in New York.

- **ELEMIS FRANGIPANI MONOI BODY OIL** A fragrant shower accessory must. Keep it housed there as the heat from the shower makes it runny and ready to roll.

- **ST. TROPEZ IN-SHOWER LOTION** The latest innovation from the fake tan geniuses at St. Tropez. Get in the shower, slather it on, get out and wait for three minutes, then jump back in and wash it off. It gives a healthy glow and you can build on the coverage each day. Especially easy for home fake tan novices like me.

- **MODELCO TAN AIRBRUSH IN A CAN** One can sells every 30 seconds since launching in 2003. It's great for face and body and has a clever 360-degree nozzle for all-over coverage.

- **PALMER'S COCOA BUTTER FORMULA WITH VITAMIN E** A household moisturising name in the US that began its life straight off the streets of Harlem. Its hot ingredient is intensely rich cocoa butter, which helps lock in moisture.

- **MOR MARSHMALLOW BODY CREAM** I was introduced to this little gem ten years ago and have been a devotee ever since. I own it in the body oil and the cream and every time I smell it, I fall in love with it all over again. It is a rich heady blend of avocado, soybean, wheatgerm cocoa butter and rosehip to nourish dry skin. On the scent front, marshmallow, peach and ginger combine for pure intoxication.

- **PRTTY PEAUSHUN** Crafted by celebrity makeup artist Bethany Karlyn, this is one of those genius body-shimmer products that just keeps on keeping on. It is shimmery and really great for legs. It's also vegan, gluten-free, fragrance-free and paraben-free.
- **JERGENS BB BODY PERFECTING SKIN CREAM** The Jergens brand has been adored worldwide since 1901 and is the number one body moisturiser in the US. My personal favourite is the BB body cream as it hides all manner of sins and leaves legs looking flawless.
- **DERMALOGICA STRESS RELIEF TREATMENT OIL** This brilliant aromatherapy-based multi-tasker is one you can mix with your favourite hand cream for an added boost. Add to the bath, slather on as a body oil or use for a stress-relieving scalp massage. The aroma (a blend of sandalwood, lavender, orange, clary sage, patchouli and ylang-ylang) is enough to radically reduce the stress metre.

THE DIGITS

- **CND SOLAROIL** One of those deskside/bedside products that you should use on a daily basis to keep cuticles in top nick.
- **NEUTROGENA NORWEGIAN FORMULA HAND CREAM** I love the story behind this hand cream: the formula came into being because hardy Norwegian fishermen had remarkably baby-soft hands, as a result of coming into contact with fish oil. Neutrogena worked this out and created a synthetic version of the fish oil as the base for their soothing hand cream, which they developed in 2000. Other ingredients include glycerine and humectants. It's genius for parched hands, rough elbows, knees and heels. You only need the tiniest amount and just one 56 gram tube lasts for more than 200 applications.

- **PHILOSOPHY FOOTNOTES FOOT SCRUB** is a great energising foot reviver.
- **AESOP RESURRECTION AROMATIQUE HAND WASH** is an exfoliating hand cleanser that smells divine and leaves hands scrupulously clean.
- **CND VINYLUX TOP COAT** Helps preserve your polish.
- **ESSIE SAND TROPEZ** The perfect, nearly nude putty shade suits every skin tone and is DBP, formaldehyde- and toluene-free. Two coats will have your nails looking polished and perfect.
- **OPI LINCOLN PARK** For a walk on the dark side, my continuous obsession is nearly pitch-black Lincoln Park – great for fingers and toes.
- **DR LEWINN'S REVITANAIL NAIL STRENGTHENER** The number one selling nail strengthener in Australia, an all-in-one base coat, top coat and treatment that helps harden, strengthen and protect nails. Everyone needs some of this action.
- **ZOYA BIG FLIPPER POLISH REMOVER PLUS** My go-to polish remover. It removes polish, preps and conditions nails and comes in the coolest dispenser.
- **DIOR CRÈME ABRICOT NAIL CREAM** A cuticle salve launched over 50 years ago, this is a darling of beauty editors the world over. It ticks all the boxes: cult, gorgeous pillbox packaging, deeply nourishing moisturiser, the perfect shade of apricot, and, what's more, it works.

MAKEUP WARDROBE

- **SHISEIDO LIQUID COMPACT IN 120** This is my constant handbag foundation companion and has been for over 30 years.
- **LANCÔME HYPNÔSE MASCARA** Mastermind mascara maker Jean-Louis Gueret created Hypnôse Doll Eyes mascara and the wand is testament to his dedication. The cone-shaped brush helps create volume, length and curl, and it's the number one mascara in Europe and the UK.

THE
ULTIMATE
EDIT

- **CHANEL LES BEIGES HEALTHY GLOW MULTI-COLOUR** The gorgeous self-stripe on this bronzer is almost too good to spoil, but once you apply it where the sun would naturally touch your face, or as a quick eyeshadow, there will be no regrets.
- **CHARLOTTE TILBURY LIPSTICK IN BITCH** Makeup artist Charlotte Tilbury can do no wrong and this lipstick is no exception. Let's just say it has joined the hallowed halls along with my other nude babies.
- **LANOLIPS RED APPLE LIP BALM** Another handbag staple, as it soothes lips and adds a punch of colour.
- **HOURGLASS ILLUSION TINTED MOISTURISER IN IVORY** I met Carisa Janes, the founder of this miraculous beauty brand, and was immediately converted to this deeply fabulous tinted moisturiser that can double as a foundation.
- **DIORSHOW BROW STYLER GEL** I am so guilty of neglecting the essential frame for the face, my brows, but I recently discovered this fab brow gel with a cleverly designed brush that leaves no hair uncoated by its gel-serum formula.
- **CLINIQUE ALMOST LIPSTICK IN BLACK HONEY** Launched in 1971, this blackened raisin lip gloss (the perfect, universally flattering blend of red, blue, orange and yellow pigments) became an instant hit. Julia Roberts won over lipstick fans around the globe when she applied Black Honey in *Stepmom* while singing 'Ain't No Mountain High Enough'.
- **LAURA MERCIER FOUNDATION PRIMER** The original Laura Mercier Foundation Primer has been around since God was a boy (well, 1995) and revolutionised foundation application as it provided the perfect silky base for flawless, longer-lasting application.

- **LAURA MERCIER CANDLEGLOW LUMINIZING PALETTE** Draws inspiration from the flattering light that twinkling candles throw, hence the name. This is one of the bang-for-your-buck palettes that has two all-over highlighters perfect for translucent spring makeup, plus four soft eyeshadow washes. There is no risk of dusty-looking skin here. This a keeper.

- **M.A.C MATTE LIPSTICK IN LADY DANGER** One of those universally flattering reds that everyone should own. I spied it on another beauty editor and immediately had to have it. The densely orange undertone makes it the perfect summer red.

- **LAURA MERCIER CAVIAR STICK** I'll take whatever colour is going. I love a smoky eye and this stick gives the best bang for your buck. It is truly foolproof.

- **BOBBI BROWN LONG-WEAR CREAM EYESHADOW IN BONE** Quite simply a genius product that I have adored for as long as it has been in existence.

- **M.A.C VIVA GLAM V** is my up-to-the-minute favourite lipstick, as I had my makeup done in store and this colour totally passed muster. This and Twig – hold on, that's two but maybe I can just count it as one.

- **M.A.C STRIPDOWN LINER** I was introduced to this at New Zealand Fashion Week and am now in love with it. I often colour my entire lip in and wear it just on its own for a matte finish or with a dash of lip gloss. There goes that customising again.

- **GIORGIO ARMANI FLUID SHEER** This is a new inclusion in the armoury and is great for luminosity. Mixing it in with a foundation or tinted moisturiser or worn just on its own, it is gold.

- **NARS THE MULTIPLE IN COPACABANA** This has made it in from the original list. Love it worn high on the cheeks.

THE
ULTIMATE
EDIT

- **BENEFIT BENETINT** Created in the 70s in San Francisco for an exotic dancer who wanted her nipples to look pinker, this is now known as a waterproof cheek and lip tint.
- **GIORGIO ARMANI LUMINOUS SILK FOUNDATION** The launch of this foundation sent shockwaves around the world, in a good way. This lightweight foundation has silky seamless coverage and my personal favourite is 4.5.
- **NARS BLUSH IN ORGASM** The name says it all. This post-coital blush launched in 1999 and instantly became a cult must-have. It graces the kits of makeup artists the world over because of its ability to blush up all skin tones. It was also the springboard for nine other Orgasm products in the range, including one of our favourites, Super Orgasm Illuminator. Worldwide, 135 units are sold every hour.
- **STILA KITTEN EYESHADOW** Another original and best with its scrumptious pinky golden tones. It has been such a hit that Stila has created a liquid eyeshadow, lip glaze, gloss and smudge pot in the same delicious hue.
- **CHANEL EYE PENCIL IN BLACK KOHL** Because you know that after nude lipstick, black eyeliner worn on the inner rim of my eyes is my poison. I love the fact that Chanel still produce the archetypal pencil variety that can be easily sharpened.
- **YSL TOUCHE ÉCLAT** There have been many pretenders to the throne but this iconic product still wears the crown when it comes to illuminating and concealing. It launched in 1992 and the pen-brush pump technique, which delivers just the right amount of product, was revolutionary. It holds the number one spot at YSL and one is sold every ten seconds globally. Touche Éclat corrects makeup smudges

and smeared eyeshadow; conceals pigmentation, blemishes and redness; and blended into the eyelid, on the brow's arch or the inner corner of the eye, it boosts radiance.

- **CHANEL ROUGE COCO SHINE IN REBEL** Gabrielle Chanel was always coming up with quotable quotes and this one is no exception. 'Since we all agree that the eyes are the mirror of the soul, why not also admit that lips are the mouthpiece of the heart?' She maintained that lipstick was a woman's primary weapon of seduction and never left the house without wearing her favourite intense vermilion red. Chanel has retailed lipsticks since 1924 and this modern, easy-to-wear rendition of Mademoiselle's favourite shade is an ultra-lightweight lipstick that is a handbag essential.

- **PRIORI COFFEEBERRY NATURAL MINERALS PERFECTING FOUNDATION** This much-loved mineral foundation is one of those revolutionary finds. Not only does it give flawless luminous coverage – great on its own or as a finishing touch to your regular liquid base – it also has other endearing qualities, including an SPF of 25 and natural ingredients. As with all mineral foundations, you need to make sure it is blended properly with a dedicated powder foundation brush (my favourite is by Eve Lom).

- **URBAN DECAY THE NAKED PALETTE** This has to be one of my all time favourites. It houses 12 seriously wearable eyeshadow colours and comes with a double-ended application brush. I am obsessed. Every single shade is a winner and the brush is great.

THE
ULTIMATE
EDIT

HAIR

- **KLORANE OAT MILK DRY SHAMPOO** A product loved by Australian women – so much so that we account for one third of total sales worldwide. That equals two cans every minute.

- **CHARLES WORTHINGTON INSTANT ROOT CONCEALER IN DARK BLONDE** A bloody lifesaver. Invariably I get to around two weeks before my next colour appointment and the grey roots start shining through. This root concealer is just that and is so easy to apply, it's ridiculous.

- **ISLES FORMULA 3-STEP SYSTEM** A cool kit with a sulphate-free Shampoo that still lathers, tick, high-octane Conditioner and astonishing Finishing Serum that protects against heat styling and UV.

- **PHYTOPLAGE PROTECTIVE SUN VEIL** Hair is very susceptible to UV damage as well, so this is a great product to protect and hydrate it.

- **DAVINES LOVE SMOOTHING SHAMPOO** Family-owned Italian hair care brand Davines comes from the exotic climes of Parma and is steeped in sustainability and coolness. It contains fig extract for moisturising, olive for cleansing and rice proteins to protect hair. And the packaging is carbon-neutral.

- **JOHN FRIEDA FRIZZ EASE ORIGINAL HAIR SERUM** This legend was also on my original list and has made it onto this one for all those amazing, de-frizzing qualities. I keep one in the glove box for those humid summer days. One is sold every two minutes around the world.

- **TERAX CREMA CONDITIONER** This product has a strong celebrity following: Gwyneth Paltrow, Meg Ryan and Demi Moore are fans. It was developed over 40 years ago and combats dryness, split ends and frizz. Its unique formula has a high pH that opens the hair cuticle to deliver protein and hydration to parched, damaged hair. Claim to fame: it works like a charm without weighing hair down.

- **L'ORÉAL PROFESSIONAL ELNETT SATIN HAIRSPRAY** The number one backstage hairspray among session stylists. For many years it was not available in Australia so stylists had to smuggle it in regularly. Its micro diffuser spray means it has a super-strong hold when needed but is so fine that it just brushes out at the end of the day.
- **CHRISTOPHE ROBIN PRICKLY PEAR MASK** Paris-based Christophe Robin is a hair colouring superstar and his bespoke range of hair products is legendary. The best seller is Prickly Pear and it regenerates the scalp and hair without weighing it down.
- **MOROCCANOIL TREATMENT OIL IN LIGHT** This is the little sister of the award-winning signature product. Its ultra-lightweight formula is perfect for fine or light-coloured hair like mine. The key ingredient is argan oil, which helps strengthen and moisturise hair while improving elasticity. It is also a great shield against environmental stresses, with optimum shine-boosting qualities that won't weigh down fine hair. The secret is less is more: on freshly washed blotted hair, apply a coin-sized amount, comb through, then style. Great also as a frizz tamer on dry hair.

FRAGRANCE

- **NASOMATTO BLACK AFGANO** I love experimenting with fragrance recommendations and was intrigued by this unisex one, which is based on hashish and was developed by nose Alessandro Gualtieri and classified as a woody oriental. I'm not sure it's for me but my sons seem to like it.

- **CHANTECAILLE TIARE** After I interviewed the incredibly chic Olivia Chantecaille, I was intrigued to try one of the Chantecaille fragrances and the heady Tiare with notes of cyclamen, lily of the valley, Tahitian tiare, jasmine, ylang-ylang, red rose and vanilla was just the ticket.

- **JULIETTE HAS A GUN LUXURY COLLECTION OIL FICTION** I always wait with bated breath for every fragrance creation from the very gifted Romano Ricci, and the relaunch of this complex fragrance, originally created as a limited edition of 999 pieces, was no exception. It has top notes of bergamot; middle notes of amber, tuberose, iris and saffronheart; and base notes of vanilla, sandalwood and papyrus oil.

- **CHANEL NO. 22** I know I keep returning to this fragrance time and time again but that it because it is part of my past and present, and will always be in my future. I think if push came to shove and I could only wear one, this would still be it. As they say: fragrance is emotion.

- **DIPTYQUE PHILOSYKOS** This reminds me of the day I visited the Diptyque store in Paris. Nothing can prepare you for how transporting it is. I adore the candles, especially Figuier, and when I wear the fig-based Philosykos, which is every day at the moment, it reminds me of my times in Paris.

- **FRÉDÉRIC MALLE PORTRAIT OF A LADY** Created by perfumer extraordinaire Dominique Ropion for Frederic Malle, this is an astonishing blend of rose essence surrounded by patchouli and smoke. Frédéric Malle, explaining why he works with Dominique Ropion, said: 'Because he is probably the most skilled perfumer today. He seems to have the best knowledge of raw materials. His technique is amazing. Dominique is always open to new ideas and this was one for sure! Other top perfumers are not always that open-minded.'

- **FRÉDÉRIC MALLE IRIS POUDRE** The unisex thing always intrigues me and this scent is no exception, with its notes of bergamot, orange, rosewood, carnation, magnolia, jasmine, violet, aldehydes, vanilla and musk. It sounds complex but the simplicity is pure joy.

- **PENHALIGON'S BLUEBELL EAU DE TOILETTE** From its beginnings in 1872, when William Penhaligon created Hammam Bouquet, Penhaligon's is now the proud possessor of two Royal Warrants and has a slew of must-have fragrances. My favourite was created in 1978 and was worn by Princess Diana. It is a delightful concoction of hyacinth, lily of the valley, jasmine and cinnamon.

- **GUERLAIN VÉTIVER** This original grassy green, woody fragrance is as modern today as it was when it launched in 1959. It has loads of sex appeal and I love its unique, zesty, just-cut-grass freshness.

- **CREED FLEURISSIMO** This intoxicating scent with notes of tuberose, Bulgarian rose, violet and Florentine iris was commissioned by Prince Rainier for Grace Kelly to wear on her wedding day in 1956. Doesn't get much more romantic that! Seems that royalty has a penchant for this fragrance, as it is said to be one of Kate Middleton's favourites too.

DEAR READER, I hope you have had as much fun reading my book as I have had writing it. The creative process has brought back so many incredible memories and reignited my passion for beauty all over again. At the risk of repeating myself, I have the luckiest, most remarkable job in the world and I plan to be a 'beauty queen' for as long as you will have me. Never fear, I will keep on searching for that perfect nude lipstick, seeking out signature scents and putting my body on the line to test drive the extremes of pleasure and pain.

Stephanie x

THE
ULTIMATE
EDIT

ACKNOWLEDGEMENTS

To begin at the beginning, I would like to thank my beloved mother, Yolande Munn, for her exceptional vocabulary and stellar mothering skills - in the reverse order of course. To my husband, Mark Darling, for having the best surname and for taking me away for our well-earned 25th wedding anniversary on a cruise from Venice to Singapore, travelling old style. The sea days on our verandah gave me the space and time to finish this book. Thank you from the bottom of my heart. To my adored family: Harrison, Jonah, Linden, Isabel and Louis. Thank you for having faith in me and being quietly proud. Thank you to Michele Neil who saved my life, literally, almost four years ago (there's another book in that). And thank you to all the truly amazing and inspiring editors and teams who I have worked with as well as the incredible PRs and beauty companies who have been at my constant beck and call. And to all those practitioners who have laid hands on me and given me so much to write about as well as holding back the hands of time.

To Marion Hume for making it all happen by setting me on my beauty path when I was at *Vogue* and to the legendary Pat Ingram who continues to watch over and care for me in my current role as beauty director at Fairfax. A huge thank you to my wonderful agent at Curtis Brown, Grace Heifetz (and to Priscilla Nielsen who introduced me), who navigated me through the process with so much care and love and helped make me a published author with the awesome Penguin Random House. Thank you to Kirsten Abbott for believing in me in the first place and to Sarah Fairhall for sensitively editing my book and making it what it is today.

Thank you to my dear Sherine Youssef, who read my book as each chapter unfolded and was my appropriateness monitor. To Shona Martyn, who has been my lifelong mentor and friend since I was a puppy journalist in my first job at *Vogue*, thank you for always being there. And last but by no means least to the gorgeous beauty posse many of whom have become my much-loved friends.

THE
ULTIMATE
EDIT